101 INTERNET MARKETING TIPS

FOR YOUR BUSINESS

Other titles by the same author

The Complete Idiot's Guide to Managing Change

The Complete Idiot's Guide to Reinventing Yourself

The Ten Minute Guide to Managing Stress

The Ten Minute Guide to Project Management

The Ten Minute Guide to Managing Time

Breathing Space

Marketing Yourself and Your Career

The Complete Idiot's Guide to Managing Stress

The Joy of Simple Living

The Complete Idiot's Guide to Managing Your Time

Marketing for the Home-Based Business

The Complete Idiot's Guide to Reaching Your Goals

Marketing Your Consulting and Professional Services

The Complete Idiot's Guide to Assertiveness

101 INTERNET MARKETING TIPS

FOR YOUR BUSINESS

*Increase Your Profits and
Stay Within Your Budget*

JEFF DAVIDSON

EP

Entrepreneur® Press

Editorial Director: Jere Calmes
Cover Design: Dunn and Associates
Composition and Production: Eliot House Productions

This publication is designed to provide accurate and authoritative information in regard to the subject matter covered. It is sold with the understanding that the publisher is not engaged in rendering legal, accounting, or other professional services. If legal advice or other expert assistance is required, the services of a competent professional person should be sought.

Library of Congress Cataloging-in-Publication Data
Davidson, Jeffrey P.
    101 Internet marketing tips for your business: increase your profits
and stay within your budget/Jeff Davidson.
    p.   cm.
  Includes index
  ISBN 1-891984-34-9
    1. Internet marketing. I. Title: One hundred one Internet marketing
tips for your business. II. Title.
  HF5415.1265 D375 2002
  658.8'4—dc21   2001053189

Printed in Canada
09 08 07 06 05 04 03 02 01   10 9 8 7 6 5 4 3 2 1

CONTENTS

ACKNOWLEDGMENTS

Thanks to subject matter experts Terry Brock, David Arnold, Bill Ringle, Rebecca Morgan, Tricia Santos, Ken Braly, Art Berg, Tony Alessandra, Nancy Roebke, Tom Antion, Jesse Wacht, Glen Christopher, Charley Morris, Dan Janal, and Ty Boyd.

Thanks also to my fine cadre of student helpers gifted in research, writing, copyediting, proofing, and all around editorial assistance, including Brian Lawler, Christie Koch, Ian Zook, Jessie Bromwell, Beth Lyn Hocutt, Tashia Zeigler, Sharon Askew, and Matt Maloney.

I would like to acknowledge Carol Susan Roth for identifying this wonderful opportunity to work with the fine folks at Entrepreneur Books. Thanks to Markman in acquisitions, Jere Calmes as Editorial Director, Kim White in marketing, and Karen Billipp at Eliot House Productions.

Thanks to the dozens of innovative entrepreneurial leaders whose examples serve as beacons to us all. Thanks to Susan Davidson for efficient word processing, and finally thanks to Valerie Davidson, age 11½, who is destined to be a superstar in using the Web for maximum impact and ultimate good.

DEDICATION

This book is dedicated to anyone who ever had the dream of being
in business for themselves, and now, because of widely available
information and communication technology,
is living that dream.

PREFACE

Before 1994, the year that Netscape's user-friendly browser starting sweeped America, chances are that you had little to do with the Internet. Now, the Internet is or is looming as an indispensable component of your company's overall marketing mix.

101 Internet Marketing Tips examines more than 100 strategies and tips that you can use to harness the Internet, and more

Any book can recommend a high-cost, high-maintenance marketing strategy—and that's what most of them do. Large organizations with deep pockets find such strategies attractive. For small businesses with neither the funds nor the desire for elaborate Web schemes, particularly firms of one to three people, this book is what the small business marketing doctor ordered.

specifically the World Wide Web (the Web). You'll learn how to market your business by taking advantage of achievable, affordable strategies for small businesses. The primary emphasis will be on low cost and no cost techniques that you can employ right away.

ULTIMATELY, BLUE SKIES

Don't let the fate of some dotcom companies in the early years of the new millennium or the campaign against terrorism distort your long-term view of the Web and of the Internet driven economy. The year 2000 witnessed the worst dip in the stock market since 1990 and the worst year ever for the Nasdaq.

As the Nasdaq composite index fell 51 percent below the indexes' highest mark in early March, and overall fell 39 pecent for the year, too many people, in too many sectors, once totally bullish and even "irrationally exuberant" about the growth of the new economy, turned about face and became equally vehement naysayers. With disturbing events of 2001, dips continued in erratic fashion. This is a new era, however, with new economic mechanisms in place (i.e., online trading and globally linked markets).

The potential growth for the "Internet economy" between now and the end of the decade, even with expensive struggle to combat terrorism worldwide, cannot be viewed with the lenses of the past. With the myriad of broadband applications in the pipeline and a grow user base, the Internet of the early 2000s will prove to be only a distant, ill-equipped ancestor of what is to come.

Small business marketers recognize that some day soon Internet access will be as common as telephone use. A study by the Pew Internet and American Life Project shows that Internet access continues to grow.

More than half of American adults have now gone online either to access the Web or send and receive e-mails. The gap between lowest income and highest income families is narrowing. Even older Americans are going online in increasing numbers each year.

Adults between the ages of 18 and 29, 75 percent of whom regularly use the Internet, and adults 30 to 49, 65 percent of whom regularly use the Internet, are the key targets for most Internet marketers. If your product(s) cater exclusively to women, minorities, or other distinct markets, increasingly these groups are on the Internet as well. Women actually use the Internet in nearly equal numbers to men.

Nearly 50 percent of Hispanics have online access, as do 43 percent of African-Americans. Moreover, racial disparities do not tend to cross categories—wealthy African-Americans are as likely to be online as wealthy Caucasians. In short, the Internet is becoming a familiar, intriguing territory for everyone.

AN INTRIGUING PLACE FOR ALL USERS

The odds are that you're intrigued by the Internet. You have favorite sites that you visit repeatedly. With literally millions more sites coming online each week, the Web has quickly become the Mecca of global information—the mother of quick and easy access to data.

Because it has grown and changed so quickly, and will continue to do so for the foreseeable future, the opportunities for you as a small business entrepreneur, understandably, have shifted from the mid-1990s, even the late-1990s, even the early-2000s! So, we will maintain a vigilant focus on marketing tips that are likely to maintain efficacy as the Internet continues to evolve.

A TEN-CHAPTER ARRAY

The strategies in this book are divided into ten chapters. Understandably, some strategies are multifaceted and achieve multiple objectives, hence they logically could appear in one chapter or another. Still, the allocations made here should suffice.

Chapter 1, *A Solid Design for Getting Online*, offers tips on developing a marketing focus, branding, learning from your peers, and maintaining an appropriate time frame, among other tips. Chapter 2, *Marketing Ideas that Mean Business*, highlights keeping abreast of new marketing ideas, naming your business, using key words, viral marketing, third-party marketing, and acquiring more than one Web site.

Chapter 3, *Basic Tools for a Booming Medium*, focuses on using sound, photographs, customized writing, images, keywords, applets, and animation to attract and retain site visitors. Chapter 4 offers an extensive look at *Site Inclusions for Striking Cybergold*, such as tips-of-the-day, tips-of-the-week, articles, booklists, and magazines lists, not to mention auto responders, surveys, quizzes, chat rooms, and forums.

What about the actual design of your Web site? That's handled in Chapter 5, *Web Site Design for the Sublime*. Topics covered there include getting help in designing your site, Web design efficiency, the need to keep it simple, offering merchandise for sale, using meta tags to your advantage, and much more. Chapter 6, *Tango With Your Customer*, presents a variety of options at your disposal for making customers feel at home at your site, and encouraging them to take advantage of it. Topics include conducting polls, offering reminder services, providing online tutorials, initiating gift registries, and donating space.

A HAPPY CUSTOMER IS A RETURNING CUSTOMER

Chapter 7, *Keeping Customers Happy*, provides insights on listening to customers, making a site more convenient, offering safe and easy online shopping, and making shopping on your site a pleasure for visitors. Chapter 8, *Keeping the Train Running*, offers advanced Web marketing ideas on such diverse topics as updating your site, using articles to attract visitors, syndicating, offering instant alerts, making your site sticky, highlighting your URL, assembling a lineup of test visitors, and more.

Each visitor to your site represents a single person, and hence, your site gets visited one person at a time even if 1,000 happen to be visiting in the same day. Chapter 9, *Delighting Visitors One at a Time*, examines how to attract single visitors through a variety of proactive strategies involving e-mail, zaplets, and mailing. Chapter 10, *Using Search Engines, Appealing to the World*, discusses the intricacies of keeping your engine rankings high so that people from all over the world can find you if you so choose. It closes with tips on making your site more internationally appealing and achieving global recognition.

THE OPPORTUNITY IN EVERY ENCOUNTER

Every time somebody encounters your URL, visits your site, or responds to an offer that you've provided through any media, you have the opportunity to develop a long-term customer. The Internet, the Web, and your Web site, in particular, are powerful tools that will help dictate the strength and future of your business.

Whether your small business is essentially a dotcom, a clicks and mortar operation, or a highly traditional business with a simple Web presence, the odds are that the Web will play an increasing role in the health and vitality of your business throughout the first decade of the 21st century.

IDEA STIMULATORS

Some of the tips presented in this book directly apply to you. However, many will simply serve as idea stimulators: You will develop variations on a theme, taking insights and observations offered here, and adapting them in a way that is right for you. In the Internet age, no one's marketing ploy, no matter how brilliantly conceived and executed, can remain a secret for long. Everyone can visit everyone else's site, so the marketing winners among small businesses in the Internet age will be those entrepreneurs who continually keep an eye out for innovative approaches.

Finding a niche, developing that niche, staying flexible, and knowing when to move on have never been more important. What works today might be old hat by tomorrow and behind the times the day after that. What worked years ago may work again depending on how it's applied.

What a time to be a small business marketer! Whether you're a veteran Web marketer, or just getting into the game, you'll find a boatload of ideas here to support your business and propel you forward on the marketing front. May your journey be exhilarating and rewarding.

—Jeff Davidson
Chapel Hill, North Carolina

INTRODUCTION

THE TRUTH IS OUT THERE SOMEWHERE

The Internet changes everything. The Internet changes nothing. Somewhere between these extremes lies the truth.

Most people, to this day, still confuse the Internet and the World Wide Web. The World Wide Web is simply a subset of the Internet. Much more traffic and many more forms of communication are transmitted over the Internet. The World Wide Web is the popular medium for business and home users, and nevertheless, has vast unreaped potential.

Shortly, instead of being accessible by handheld computers, cell phones, and other devices, the Web will enable you to use your own cell phone to listen to music stored on a friend's computer, access your own computer remotely, and even give you a call on your home phone or pager when an important e-mail arrives for you.

Never mind if the first wave of the dotcom craze is over, or that investors are abandoning the Nasdaq, or analysts proclaim that nothing exciting is coming out of the Web these days. The Internet is still in its infancy stages, and the Web that you now know will look nothing like the Web in a few years hence. The first wave of the Internet was essentially a medium for viewing content, buying products, playing games, and sending messages. Not bad, but not all-embracing either.

FROM INFANCY TO ADOLESCENCE

Before the blink of an eye, the Internet will progress to adolescence and take on a completely different character. The watch word will be service. Travel sites, for example, will be able to coordinate the arrangements you make online with your calendar on your handheld computer and then instantaneously initiate e-mail to your coworkers, families, and friends about up-coming travel.

Regardless of the ultimate fate of Napster, one of the many lessons that we learn from the groundswell of support Napster received from site users is that the old, powerful, established order does not go away quietly. Even if the record industry is able to generate more revenues and higher profitability as a result of per song fees or monthly subscriptions via music sharing services, it may take years before they deal with it. The powers that be are wedded to CDs, packaging, shipping, warehousing, and the industrial age trappings that are part and parcel of the world in which they dwell. They fear recording artists will by-pass them altogether.

The power structure would prefer to ignore that music is now digital. This is a clear case of the Internet irrevocably changing an entire industry. Once people discover the awesome power of saving, storing, arranging, manipulating, and controlling their song base, they will never return to what came before. Yet, this is only beginning to sink in to record executives' minds. If you're an established business entity, what changes may be in store for your industry as a result of the Internet? Contemplate the inevitabilities and you can stay ahead in the game.

The stock market vicissitudes of dotcom companies notwithstanding, the power and potential of your ability to harness the Internet is limited only by your imagination. While it's not practical for most entrepreneurs to emulate the moves of an Amazon.com or Yahoo.com, there certainly are lessons and insights that can be drawn from the biggest and best of the Net.

WEB SITES WORTH A RETURN VISIT

What lessons from the Internet success stories can be drawn, right off the bat? When you find an information-rich Web site you can rely on, naturally you're more prone to make a return visit. Everyone who's regularly on the Web has his or her own favorites. Here are some ideas on what makes a site worth bookmarking and visiting regularly:

- *Periodic updates.* Updates that offer some key changes on at least the opening screen, once a week, once a day, or more often.
- *Up-to-the-moment updates.* Updates presenting trends, breakthroughs, or results; becoming known as the place to visit each day for news or public service messages.
- *Quickly engaging.* A site that encourages immediate participation; giving visitors choices, the opportunity to vote for something, or the chance to send an opinion.
- *Online tutorial.* Teaching visitors something; offering short, to-the-point instructions or guidance on a topic of interest.
- *For members only.* Featuring "members only" options requiring a password to enter.
- *An article series.* Giving readers information in serial form.
- *Survey or polling results.* Publishing the results of polls.

- *Rating guides to products or services*. Categorizing hotels, airlines, airports, audio/visual equipment, and so on.
- *Review service*. A site that reviews movies, books, software, programs, courses, or the Web itself.

One way to determine the most useful Web site for you is to ask others what they have found to be effective.

THE BEST LEAVE CLUES

Good Web sites have common features. Sites that offer some or all of the items listed below help you to optimize your time online.

- *Keep visitors from getting lost*. A good Web site includes multiple links that take you back to the home page, to the previous page, or another value-packed page of your choice.
- *Flexibility of movement*. This feature ensures that you can quickly return to something familiar and comfortable or move on to something else.
- *Displays appropriate graphics*. Many Web sites are works of art by master graphic artists. Smaller graphics and text-only hyperlinks, however, enable you to navigate much faster.
- *Includes multiple contact links*. Good sites contain clear links that point you to contact information such as e-mail, fax, snail mail address, and phone numbers, if appropriate.
- *Maintains a visitor-focus*. A good site focuses on the visitor's needs, ensuring that the most valuable information with no slow loading graphics can be directly accessed.

The Jupiter Research Company did a study to determine the leading reasons that people use the Internet to help manage their personal finances. Whether or not you are in the investment industry, the findings are most illuminating since presiding over one's own money is about as core a concern as one can have. The chart below indicates the percentage of those surveyed saying that the following factors are important:

Access to information	68%
Saving time	62%
Can manage my account in off hours	62%
No need to visit street location	52%
Cost savings	52%
Greater independence	47%
Paperless statements	30%
Real time customer service reps	20%

It's not surprising that the top three factors are having access to information, saving time, and taking control. Add in having an enjoyable or entertaining experience and you have the essence of what most visitors want most of time.

ON THE BLEEDING EDGE?

Sticking to the basics while adding some innovations has worked well for many sites. Do you, however, need to be on the cutting edge of Internet service delivery to be successful, or are there inherent traps in getting too far in front too fast?

To those would-be small business Internet marketer pacesetters: While it's admirable to be the first in your niche to offer a particular product, service, or unique Web feature, be wary of being too far in front of the pack. Being on the bleeding edge is always more costly and more risky than the leading edge.

If you're attempting to create a new industry on the Web, forget it. For every Amazon, eBay, and Travelocity, there are thousands of sites that have disappeared. The entrepreneur had either grandiose schemes about what the Internet could do for their business or was so far in front of the times that there was no market.

In its infancy, the Web was relatively low cost. In its adolescence, there are more services for fees. The wise small business Internet marketer will begin positioning themselves now to offer services for fees. People will willingly pay for them because the convenience will equal more and offset the cost. Steve Ballmer, CEO of Microsoft says, "Web sites will be expected to have the best attributes of software. Software will be expected to have the best attributes of the Web."

Think of the word-processing database management spread sheets software that you currently use. Now, suppose that your site encompasses the flexibility and capabilities of such commonly used applications. Your typical visitors' experiences will be greatly enhanced because they will be able to do so much more. Like Amazon.com does now with its independent booksellers, you will be able to manage the entire transaction history for your customers right online.

Every time a customer orders from you can be accumulated for them at a URL you provide. Hence, with the click of a mouse they can get complete records for tax purposes, historical analysis, and current comparisons. For business to business transactions, the ability to manage your client or customer's accounts for them will become a very attractive feature of doing business with you. It could prove to be an important component of your company's overall marketing strategy.

Turn now to Chapter 1 to explore a sound approach for getting online and making the most of it.

1

A SOLID DESIGN FOR GETTING ONLINE

The Web-based economy, predictably, has become a battleground of fierce competitors. With so many entrepreneurs launching so many new companies, it's important to plan ahead to succeed. Yet most Web start-ups basically dive right in and try to develop marketing strategies on the run.

In his own Internet start-up experiences, Marc Andreessen, founder of Loudcloud, witnessed a lot of abandonment of the plan-ahead attitude of the business world. Unlike those around him who were also starting Internet businesses, Andreessen founded Loudcloud with a more traditional plan: he painstakingly constructed the business model; he skillfully interviewed and recruited employees; and he thoroughly completed the infrastructure before launching any operations.

As Andreessen said, "That way we could hit the ground running and beat anybody else with the same idea to the market." He saw that success came with a well-developed

> The key to success is to be more accurate than your competitors in carefully executing your idea and promoting your business.

business model: "If your model fails to align your goals with those of your customer...then it's going to be difficult."

Even when taking any existing small business or entrepreneurial idea to the Web, it's necessary to think and plan ahead. Do your research. First, determine your business model. What is your budget? How much can you spend to set up a Web site and how much can you budget for advertising and marketing? The answers to these questions determine how you can proceed and take your business into the new Web-based market.

> Starting a Web-based business requires forethought and planning. Although the dotcom world moves quickly, the most successful Internet marketers will think ahead of time and consider how they can best serve their customers.

As Andreessen says, "Right now thousands of entrepreneurs are trying to think up the 'Next Big Thing.'" So, which business will survive? The ones whose founders continue to think, plan, and change for the future.

FIND A NICHE AND FILL IT

Don't fret if you're not the first in the marketplace or even the first in a highly selected, focused niche area. Concentrate on being first and best in an area in which you can dominate. Perhaps you wish to appeal to a specific, narrowly focused geographical segment of the population or a demographic segment of the market, such as women ages 35 to 52.

As with all marketing strategies, the more narrowly you can focus on a particular segment of a larger market, the faster and easier you'll be able to penetrate that market. Upon continued success, you can expand your focus a little at a time, all the while knowing you can remain comfortable with your strategy and pacing.

With corporate giants such as Amazon.com and Barnes and Noble's online division as its competitors, who isn't amazed that Powells.com can keep afloat in the online bookstore market? How can such a virtual no-name bookseller turn a profit against those giants? It's relatively easy, because Powells.com, the bricks and clicks store based in Portland, Oregon, actually targets a different market.

While the big guys make traditional merchandise offerings, Powells' bookstores cater to more specific literary tastes, and so does its online business. Age-old marketing wisdom tells us that success comes in finding a lucrative niche. Once you pinpoint a market, you can provide your customers what they want and then make a profit. With lower overhead and advertising costs, Web-based businesses have the ability to target a particular niche with fewer expenditures than ever. The more you target the market, the lower the marketing and advertising costs.

On average, Powells advertising costs each year are only 1 percent of their sales. Instead of advertising all over, Powells targets the intellectual readership in publications such as *Mother Jones* and the *Utne Reader*. In comparison, Amazon spends 10 percent of sales on advertising in their attempt to reach the masses. Thus far Amazon has lost money each year, while Powells turns a decent profit.

In a similar niche-savvy business venture, Kurt Andersen launched Inside.com in May 2000. The site features the latest breaking news in the media and entertainment business. For a small subscription fee, readers can log on for a daily dose of the latest "dish" of entertainment and media gossip.

Previously, no other Web-based publication specialized in bringing up-to-date information on entertainment. So, in a business thriving on media attention, this e-publication certainly satisfies an existing niche in the market.

The tactic is simple, but the results produce the kind of success that keeps Web-based businesses afloat. Find a niche in a particular market, serve it well, and chances are your customers will support your business in wondrous ways.

BRANDING ON THE INTERNET

When it comes to the Internet, marketing terminology is loosely applied. A brand, for example, is a signifying name or symbol designed so that others can easily recognize the goods and/or services of a vendor and tell the difference from one vendor's goods and services over another.

Often, the term *brand* is narrowly applied, such as when it's equated with a tag line, a logo, or a design. Frequently, when entrepreneurs refer to the word brand, they are employing a short cut for the term *brand equity*. Brand equity refers to the positive and negative connotations associated with a product and/or service. It also refers to anything emblematic that it produces or services such as a name, design, or symbol.

Entrepreneurs successful in building brand awareness recognize that it requires a wide range of activities, time, and effort in support of an overall strategy.

Traditional marketing activities, which can be costly, such as nonInternet advertising, public relations, and specific or limited marketing campaigns are generally needed to develop brand awareness.

In his book *eBrands*, author Phil Carpenter observes that "the strongest Internet brands are like landslides. As they begin to pick up speed, they gain mass, then more speed, then more mass, until soon little can stand in their way."

As part of their awareness-building efforts, savvy Internet marketers do everything in their power to communicate to the market the momentum behind their brands—most often through public relations, Carpenter observes. Once they cut a big distribution deal, they are out talking about it. When they hit the "X million customers served" mark, they tell the industry.

Effective Internet marketers also use momentum to diminish business barriers, he says. They more easily attract strategic partners to develop alliances. Once customers perceive the company to be a winner, this strengthens the overall perceived quality of the brand.

KEY COMPONENTS TO INTERNET SUCCESS

Carpenter cites several components to successful Internet marketing. Among the most relevant to small business entrepreneurs are:

- Building brand awareness

- Cultivating customer commitment

- Developing an intimate knowledge of the market and customer

- Propagating a reputation for excellence

- Delivering outstanding value

Each of the above recommendations are the same things that you do to market effectively *independent* of the Internet and, indeed, as if the Internet never existed.

Rather than seeking to do everything on your own, find willing partners, a theme explored throughout the book. If you are a chiropractor, instead of attempting to write oodles of content for your site, add some of your own content, but also solicit the input of qualified nutritionists, exercise physiologists, and certified massage therapists to provide you with high level material. This creates the win-win situation in which your site features well-rounded information, and the contributors receive kudos and a hyperlink. Likewise, you may have an article or two to submit to your content alliance partners.

By any analysis, wise use of the Internet will be a major component in the long-term success of large and small businesses. Mark Barrenechea, a senior executive at Oracle, says, "It is no longer a choice: no matter what the nature of your business, you need to leverage the power of the Internet or risk going bust."

START NOW, REAP SOON

In the past, putting your business on the Web meant investing thousands in finding a domain, retaining a Web designer to construct a site, and learning to manage all the aspects of a Web store. New Web commerce services offer site construction and management tools that cater well to the interests of small businesses. For the small business entrepreneur, getting online can be simple and inexpensive.

Three Web sites, Freemerchant.com, Bigstep.com, and eCongo, offer Web-store hosting—a service that costs nothing. These sites allow companies to take their businesses online without the hefty start-up expenses. These new companies offer many of the same amenities provided by more expensive Web storefront servers. Using these services, along with other successful marketing strategies, a small business can easily get online and test the waters of Web commerce.

Each site provides simple site-building tools for designing and publishing pages, expert inventory management, and accounting services. Freemerchant.com even offers eBay auctioning for slow-moving merchandise.

Despite all of the freebies, these companies do require paid services for items such as credit-card processing. Freemerchant.com is the only one of the three that does not offer a particular set of required services, and instead allows the merchant to choose. The relatively cheap services are a great way to expand your business online.

Do merchants like these services? Sue Schwartz launched a discount specialty yarn outlet using Freemerchant.com. During the first month her sales reached $2,500. Schwartz particularly cited the eBay clearance option and customer mailing list features as big bonuses in the free Web-store service.

Along with services described, there are other Web-store hosting services that can take orders, verify credit cards, and keep an eye on your inventory for reasonable monthly fees. Top-rated companies for providing such services include: BuyItOnline, Storesense.com, Yahoo! Store, Amazon.com, and zShops.

Services provided by these companies vary widely, from basic Web storefront construction to added fee options, such as Storesense.com's

"Supplier Connect" service, which connects your inventory needs to suppliers, allowing you to authorize direct shipments to customers. Whichever you choose, your business gets online with relatively little pain to you or your budget.

DESIGNED TO BE USEFUL AND PROFITABLE

Budget adequate time to ensure that your Web site is constructed to be useful, as well as profitable. With the hype about the piles of money that some vendors have made on the Internet, you may be ready to roll out a new process or service online, thinking that all you have to do is hire a few programmers to get on the Web. Often it takes time to figure out what needs to be done and how to work out all the bugs once the programs are written. Also, make sure that your customers can benefit from the new features you implemented.

Dan Caulfield learned about the difficulties of technology while putting his job placement service online. His company, hirequality.com, maintains a database of people with military experience to help match job-seekers with recruiters. His goal was to get this database on the Web so that recruiters could search the database themselves for a fee.

Caulfield had great success when putting up a Web site for the company a few years earlier. A later decision to integrate a Web-based system with the legacy database already in place, however, was a much more complicated operation. He began to run into problems with the project.

"We expected to put our system on the Internet so that people would be able to use it intuitively and quickly—and get the same kind of productivity gains that we got over the past three years. That didn't happen. The legacy database was cumbersome. We almost had to rewrite five years of code to make this work on the Web with multiple users.

Taking a client/server system and porting it to an Internet model was hard," he said in a February 2000 *Inc.* magazine article.

Once Caulfield had the database on the Web and it was functioning properly, he wondered why customers were not using the site. It proved to be difficult to use. "The system was not intuitive," he said. The project was delayed again as programmers went back to the drawing board to come up with an easier user interface.

Caulfield advises that business owners budget for more start-up time than initial estimates. "Plan time for technology that doesn't go as smoothly as you'd like. Give yourself an extra 30 days before you roll something out."

H aving your site up and running is an important priority, but be sure that all aspects of the project are carefully planned. You don't want to sacrifice quality for speed.

OLD PROBLEM, BETTER SOLUTION

Kaleil Isaza Tuzman, CEO of GovWorks.com, was one of the first to tap into the consumer-to-government market. Tuzman realized that the existing method for paying taxes and government fines, such as parking tickets, was inefficient, to say the least. So, he developed a way to make the system work better. His Web site allows consumers to access the government online. For a fee, visitors can take care of their business with the government from their home or office.

Considering that the term "red-tape" has its roots in bureaucracies, Tuzman's innovative Web site has the potential to revolutionize how consumers interact with the government. The key to Tuzman's success lies in his understanding that nearly any service can be adapted to the Web.

PAINLESS LEARNING FROM PEERS

One of the easiest ways to effectively market your business, on the Web or anyplace else, is to learn from your peers. Often, entrepreneurs branch out on their own, feeling as if they have to know it all and build a business alone. This is erroneous thinking that can lead to wasted time, energy, and funds.

To learn about key sites that you might not otherwise discover, find others who are willing to "trade" key site finds with you. Some potential traders are your peers, clients or customers, and Web specialists.

You instantly and automatically gain access to some of the best and brightest marketing ideas available if you affiliate with the most successful people in your industry or line of work. Fortunately, there are a variety of readily available resources that will help you indicate key associations, trade groups, professional societies, and other associations of your peers. These include such helpful directories as:

- *Leadership Directories' Association* Yellow Book—the cream of the crop with photos of the top officers and department listings. Call 212-627-4140, extension 3305.
- Omnigraphic's *Directory of Associations.*
- *National Trade and Professional Associations.*
- *State and Regional Associations.*

All of these are located in the reference section of any city or academic library. By turning to the indices of these directories and finding your industry or profession, you can locate several, if not dozens, of potential groups with which you can affiliate. You can hobnob with the movers and shakers in your field if you attend meetings of professional groups, which includes their annual convention or conference, quarterly meetings, regional meetings, or state chapter meetings. If you decide to participate in a meaningful way, you will realize how important it is to network with the top dogs in your industry.

Also, you will want to subscribe to the association's or organization's quarterly or monthly magazine or newsletter. You may discover the online magazines and listserves of your group, step into the online chat rooms, participate in forums, and in many other ways participate in the exchange of ideas that is so fundamental to the success of solo-entrepreneurs.

Once you have gotten onto the wavelength of what is tried and true, or new and forthcoming within your industry, don't merely imitate or emulate what is already being done—innovate!

Find new ways to use emerging technologies, proven strategies, and effective techniques. Because everyone in your industry handles a certain type of feature on his or her Web site in one manner, doesn't mean you have to do it, too.

Pay attention to your competitors' techniques and learn from them, so that you can then improvise, innovate, and even escalate! Your peers can give you a continual Web marketing education that will help you flourish.

Still, in this dynamic world of marketing, nothing stays the same for long. Even if you happen to lead the field in one particular area, you can count on your peers to catch up with you soon—whatever you offer on the Web can be viewed by your competitors.

WHO TO TURN TO

In tapping your peers for help, seek out successful entrepreneurs who *want* to share advice with you on how they became more successful both online and off. People are more likely to give when they can receive something in exchange. To create better, more beneficial contact relationships and associations, figure out exactly with whom those relationships, contacts, and associations need to be.

First, *who* is it that you think you need to know to obtain the advice you're seeking? Is it a competitor, an owner of a site that you admire, or simply someone who has good, general knowledge of e-commerce?

After deciding who you need to know (either in general or a specific person), decide *what* fields of business you need to have associations with. For example, if you decide that you want to find people who can offer good advice on how to sell to a younger consumer base, it would probably be more beneficial to find people in the video game or skateboarding industries than in the gardening industry. This is not to say that some kids aren't into gardening.

Next, decide *where* you are looking to expand (if you are looking). Choose new markets or new target-audiences. For example, are you a clothing company looking to reach an older crowd or are you looking to have more young golfers visit your site? This will help you further refine your search for new associations and allow you to specify with whom you have relationships.

Finally, decide *how* you are going to find these people. One suggestion is to visit news groups of other entrepreneurs and post requests for advice. Find out where these people are, either online or off, and begin to mingle with them. Find out what you could offer to them in exchange for their help. Maybe you could place an ad for their site on your site in exchange for them doing the same for you. The method you choose needs to be specific to your goal.

VISIT COMPETITORS' SITES OR BE GONE

Before the Web, it made sense to review your competitors' yellow page ads, obtain whatever brochures and literature that you could, and seek to understand their overall marketing strategy. Even if you didn't engage in these activities, it's likely that some of your competitors were doing so and learning from you!

Since the Web has become a showcase arena for marketing businesses, you can still keep up with your competitors' marketing strategies. It pays for you to set up a special section of folders or bookmarks on your hard drive that contain information on key competitors, as well as suppliers and others who have an impact on your industry or profession.

Once you've assembled this compendium, visit all of your competitors' Web sites to update your information at least once a month. If you are too busy to visit these sites on your own at least monthly, then assign the task to a savvy staff member.

Fully explore competitors' Web sites, try to understand the rationale behind their formats, and even test-drive their systems. For example, if a competitor has a shopping cart, run through the mechanics of what it is like to make an order using that cart. You can always cancel at the last minute.

The tips, insights, and targeted information that you could acquire as a result of such visits are simply too valuable to leave unexplored.

While it may not be practical to add all of the wonderful features to your site that you see on your competitors' sites, it is good to know what is being offered and carefully plan your strategy as to what you will offer.

One of the many unique and fascinating aspects of the Web is that all industries continue to raise the bar, because within any industry competitors can easily keep tabs on what everyone else is doing.

2

MARKETING IDEAS THAT MEAN BUSINESS

An extreme challenge of marketing via the Internet is coping with the dynamics of its growth rate. Based on research conducted by Google.com, an astounding 70-plus percent of Web pages are less than one year old as of 2001, and more than 89 percent are less than one to two years old as reported by the Web servers. (The actual age can be greater.) This data emphasizes that for the foreseeable future the potential competitors for the time and attention of Web site visitors will continue to explode in number.

Even if your site's been up for three to five years, all other things being equal, your ability to attract first-time visitors becomes increasingly difficult. Web surfers simply have too many alternatives, regardless of what product or service you are offering. Hence, the need to clearly establish a market niche. Consider the following:

- Who are you trying to reach?

- What is your message?
- What is your goal?

Anything less than careful consideration of these issues is likely to result in your site becoming another of the multi-millions that happen to be online.

KEEP TABS ON NEW WEB MARKETING IDEAS

Fortunately, you don't have to reinvent the wheel, be overwhelmed, or be run over by it, when it comes to Web marketing techniques. While you want your site to be somewhat unique and appear innovative, you certainly can draw upon the insight, wisdom, and experience of those who are experts at Web marketing. Hence, you may wish to bookmark a number of sites that cover the "Web marketing beat."

One such site is knowthis.com, a virtual library of Web marketing techniques maintained by KnowMarketing.com. *Advertising Age* maintains a useful site at Adage.com, which always contains a variety of fresh ideas and perspectives, as does *AdWeek* at AdWeek.com.

On the direct marketing side of the ledger, *DirectMarketing Online* at DirectMarketing-Online.com and *DirectMarketing News* at Dmnews.com expertly cover the field of direct marketing. To stay abreast of developments in the field of marketing research, check out the Marketing Research Association's site at MRA-Net.org or the E-Marketers Site, EMarketer.com.

Many professional associations maintain comprehensive Web sites that will give you tips and ideas about marketing effectively online. Examples of these include the Business Marketing Association site, Marketing.org, the American Marketing Association's site at AMA.org, and the Internet Advertising Bureau at IAB.net. Each offers Web sites that are in themselves a virtual smorgasbord of ideas for Web marketers.

On occasion, simply visit one of the large search engines and type in the key words "Web marketing" or "Web marketing techniques" and a variety of links will appear; some of these will lead you to Web sites that are loaded with more ideas about effective Web marketing.

THE NAME GAME

Potential customers navigate the Web so quickly today that unless your business is blessed with a name that they can easily remember and find, you're likely to be passed over. While it might sound high-minded to call your company "The Apex Project" or "Fortanic," all you're doing with these kinds of names is increasing the odds that denizens of the Web won't find you, or if they do, won't remember you.

It's acceptable when a huge, multinational company chooses to create a name, develop an image, and establish a position that essentially holds known intrinsic meaning. Nissan, Lucent, Compaq, and Cisco all fit the bill. When you think about it, the names alone convey nothing. By spending a lot of money, working distribution channels, and exerting their influences around the globe, however, these names easily conjure up images among the consuming public.

As for your small business, pick a name that is short, easily remembered, and conveys information to parties who have never heard of you. Great examples include Earthlink.com, estamps.com, Ticketron.com, and PlanetRX.com. With these, the typical Net user knows instantly, or can figure out in seconds, what is behind the name.

Near great names include those that conjure up some kind of image, but take a little more work to understand and remember. An example of this is MySimon.com, which uses memory identification, because presumably people know about the childhood game. Another example is MentorU.com, an online university of mentors.

Amazon.com is an example of a site name that doesn't stand alone. Sure, people know that it is the earth's largest online bookstore. However, taken for its name only, one would be inclined to think that it's about a river in Brazil, a tribe of highly athletic women, or has something to do with South America. The popular search engines such as Yahoo.com, Excite.com, Lycos.com, and AltaVista.com, are excellent examples of online companies whose names in and of themselves convey nothing about the service when one hears of them for the first time.

The small business entrepreneur, especially in the start-up phase, needs to take heed from some recent successes. PayMyBills.com, Travelocity.com, and Etrade.com, are the types of examples to follow. If you are starting to offer PC repair in the local area, experiment with a variety of URLs, such as RepairYourPC.com, IfixPC's.com, PCWorks.com, WorkingComputers.com, and PCFriend.com.

If you are a trainer, consultant, or professional speaker and will be delivering some portion of your services over the Web, consider possibilities, such as Etrainer.com, WebConsultation.com, Web Speaker.com, WebTraining.com, WebPresentation.com, Ispeaker.com, or Online Consultant.com. If you're in any kind of delivery and supply business, take a lesson from 1-800-FLOWERS.com and experiment with potential names, such as 1-800-delivery.com, 1-800WeDeliver.com, 1-800 InAJiffy.com, and 1-800YourOrder.com. Or, consider possibilities such as DinnerToGo.com. Since access to your Web site is not dependent on case-sensitive letters before the dotcom, dotorg, or dotnet, accent the names that compose your URL as shown in this suggestion.

LONG NAMES CAN WORK WONDERS

Site names with compound words can work well. The *Wall Street Journal's* opinionjournal.com comes to mind. While the name is long, it is easily remembered and easily bookmarked. My own site *BreathingSpace.com* is named after my principal book and the name of my company. I am told it's easy to remember, hence easy to find.

Your own name as a Web site can work well for marketing purposes, however, unless your name is slightly unusual, the letters have probably already been taken. By linguistic quirks of fate, the more unusual your name or the spelling of your name, the more likely that your name as a domain can still be registered, and the more easily you can be found by search engines.

Products or services with distinct but memorable names can also be found more easily in search engines. If you load up your product with digits and technical sounding terms people will have a harder time finding it.

When advertising your Internet site, either online or offline, it is important to develop a campaign that will set your site apart from the millions of other Web sites. Two easy ways of doing so are to make your Web address easy to remember or relevant to what your site is offering, as previously discussed, and to put your company name and URL on every possible thing that you can.

NAMES THAT RESONATE

Here's one more look at choosing a name that supports your marketing efforts. With more than one million other Web sites on the

Internet, it is vital to find a URL, regardless of length, that will stick out in the minds of Internet users. Make sure it is easy to remember and spell. There are a couple of ways to do this. Make your URL (even if it is only a link to your actual site) unique and relevant to what you are offering on your site. For example, Bill Ringle, a professional business speaker, has a Web site called BillRingle.com. Therefore, if people want to know more about who he is and what he offers, all they have to do is know his name.

It's prudent to make the name you choose unambiguous and a phonetic match with its spelling. You do not want your site to sound like one thing but be spelled differently. For example, Ecolab (a large chemical company) has a Web site at ecolab.com. It's spelled like it sounds.

> If customers have to excessively search for your site they may never find it or they may be so frustrated that their first impression is a negative one.

If you're starting in business or are a ten-year veteran, the name you choose, particularly in the Internet age, becomes extremely important—much more so than in prior eras. A housekeeping service in Canton, Michigan calls itself The Sweeping Beauties. Thus, the Internet site Sweepingbeauties.com becomes an instant memory hook. Munchkin University in Redding, California is a day-care center and preschool for two to five year olds. Munchkin.com is not hard to remember and not hard to find.

CREATING MEMORY HOOKS

A Memory Hook is a four to seven word phrase that encapsulates the essence of a business in a way that customers and prospects can easily remember.

Once you devise a memory hook, you can use it on your printed literature and, in particular, on the opening screen of your Web site. A long-winded explanation on creating memory hooks is not as effective as simply supplying you with excellent examples from which you may draw ideas for your own.

Andrew's Scottish Motel	Our Hotel Is Your Castle
Anakopoulous Bakery	Baklava Never Had It So Good
Bed and Breakfast International	Sleep Cheap, Eat Healthy
Bearsford Hotels	When You Can Bear to Stay at the Best
California State Railroad Museum	We've Been Working on the Railroad
Catering With Style	Tummy Yummies
Celebrity Speakers Bureau	Helping You to Draw a Crowd
Celia's Party Time Inc	We Do Hardy Parties
Cornucopia Communications	You Say It, We'll Spray It
Coronado Catering Company	Cutting Edge Culinary
Executive Suites	Everything the Way You Want It
Gloria Young's Champagne Cavern	An Educated Pallet Is Our Best Customer

Ghirardelli Chocolate Company	Chocolate So Good It's Sinful
Golden Brand's Bottling Company	Bottled to Be the Best
Santa Rosa Conference and Visitors Center	Sleepy Pearl of the Pacific
Green Valley Plant Rental	We Grow It, You Show It
Hamburger Harry's	Burgers Baked in Heaven
Hawaii Vacations Unlimited	We'll Lei One on You
Hyde Street Seafood House & Raw Bar	For Fresher Seafood You'll Have to Jump in the Bay
Cathy's Yosemite Bed and Breakfast	Wake Up in Wonderland
Landmark Vineyards	Fine Vines, Exquisite Wines
Marydale Vineyards	Eat, Drink, and Be at Marydale
Pier 39	39 Reasons to Go Shopping
Reservations Tonight	Tickets on Demand
Sanchez's Mexican Buffet	A Fiesta for the Famished
San Francisco Boys' Choir	Sweet Sounds of Youth
Scott's Seafood Grill and Bar	Seafood to Savor
Shannon Court Hotel	Where Irish Eyes Are Smiling
Signs America	You Say It, We'll Display It
Stormy Leather	Leather Never Better
Town House Motel	Our House Is Your House

Your memory hooks phrase could then be the basis of a URL in addition to all of the traditional marketing maneuvers.

INITIATING MORE THAN ONE WEB SITE

Suppose you offer products and services at your principal Web site, but people might be apt to find you based on your name or your product and service offerings. As a case in point, at my principal site BreathingSpace.com, I offer information about my speeches, books, tapes, articles, and other informational resources.

Frequently, people don't remember the name of my site, but they might remember my name. Hence, I acquired the site JeffDavidson.com. Since I have this alternative site, I greatly increase the probability that people who want to find BreathingSpace.com will do so.

Suppose somebody goes to a search engine, can't remember my principal site, but types in my name, Jeff Davidson. What are they likely to find? They will get JeffDavidson.com and they might even see BreathingSpace.com. The point is that by acquiring a second site, in this case using my full name, I dramatically increased the probability that those who are looking for me will find me.

Likewise, I have gone ahead and secured sites for individual book titles. One example is my book *The Joy of Simple Living*, published by Rodale Press and one of my best sellers. I have secured the site JoyofSimpleLiving.com. I have also had business cards and literature designed that include that site name. If someone types in JoyofSimpleLiving.com they will get information on the book and, like my JeffDavidson.com site, they will find multiple links to my BreathingSpace.com site. I have also acquired DynamicSpeaker.com, GeneralSession.com, and LuncheonSpeaker.com, among others.

T he cost of acquiring and registering sites has dropped dramatically. You cannot afford not to have alternative sites that help visitors to ultimately find what they are seeking.

As browsers become more sophisticated, many people bypass search engines and simply type in the character string of key words on the browser's search line. If someone types in Jeff Davidson, in this case correctly guessing I might have such a Web site, the World Wide Web signifier (www), the type of domain (dotcom), and the http designation all get filled in and the visitor is directly brought to JeffDavidson.com.

In your own business, think about alternative sites that you could acquire that would help visitors to quickly arrive at your principal site. If you run an auto repair shop, and it is named after you, such as John's Auto Repair, could you acquire sites that have your town followed by auto repair? Or use CarFix.com, WeFixCars.com, RepairAuto.com, or AutoRepairSpecialists.com. The value of acquiring even one new customer per year as a result of registering one additional site more than pays for itself.

SPECIALIZE YOUR ADVERTISING MARKET

Once you have the right name for your site or sites, it makes sense to derive the most mileage from them. Robert Kelly is the founder of CountryWatch.com, located in Houston, Texas. His company provides specialized economic and political information about 191 nations and is ideal for business people looking to initiate business deals with international firms.

CountryWatch.com is the main provider of worldwide financial and cultural information for the search engine AltaVista. Country

Watch.com is averaging over 200,000 page views a month and is sharing ad revenue with the search engine. Advertisers will pay more when they know more about the audience.

When someone clicks on CountryWatch to acquire information about a particular nation, such as China, advertisers can predict some things about the person's interests. They are probably in business with interests in China and international travel. The banner ads at the top of the screen are likely to be for business-related products, Chinese language tapes, travel sites that can sell airline tickets and hotel reservations, and other similar sites. Advertisers know that a person will be more likely to explore a banner ad if they can perceive some immediate use for it. So, companies target people who go to CountryWatch.com.

What does this mean for your small business? Look for sites that are likely to have the type of visitors who would like to use your goods and services. If you are a wedding photographer, then look for local sites that have information about local weddings or receptions. Many brides—and grooms-to-be—will look at that site while they are planning the big event. Perhaps you could buy some ad space at the top of the screen and advertise your services.

Look for beneficial partnerships and relationships with other companies that have Web sites, products, and services that complement yours.

A person that owns a charter-fishing service at the beach might partner with a local hotel owner. The charterer could put a free link to the hotel on their Web site, if the hotel owner does the same on the hotel site. People coming into town to stay at the hotel would see the link, perhaps explore it, and decide they want to do a little fishing on their vacation. Likewise, a person coming to the beach to fish will check out the hotel link, since he or she may be looking for a place to stay.

These reciprocal links are often an effective and free way to get the word out about your business to a specific audience more likely to use your goods and services than the general population. By focusing your marketing campaign, you can significantly increase the return on your marketing expenditures.

KEYWORDS: A KEY TO WEB SITE MARKETING

"Everyone agrees that keywords are the key to an effective marketing campaign using search engines," says Glen Christopher, a professional speaker, author, and Internet trainer at caal.com. Since graduating from Cornell University School of Engineering 23 years ago, Christopher has been designing, installing, and managing networked computer systems. "There are many keys to using keywords that can enhance or limit your success," he says. One key to success is adding an "s."

Christopher advises that your strategic keywords always be at least two or more words long, to make keyword phrases. "Usually, too many sites will be relevant for a single word, such as *speaker*, as in my profession. Competing with Web sites featuring *speakers* from JBL, Sony, and RCA dilutes your efforts. This kind of competition means your odds of success are lower," he advises. "Don't waste your time fighting the odds. Pick phrases of two or more words, and you'll have a better shot at success."

Goto.com's keyword database at inventory.go2.com/inventory/Search_Suggestion.jhtml, is an interesting and useful tool that helps you formulate phrases of two or more words. This keyword database service helps buyers select keyword phrases for Goto.com.

The database offers statistics about search phrases that include your keywords, and also tells you the number of times each phrase was searched during the prior month. Use it. Then you can apply this knowledge base to the seven popular search engines:

- AltaVista.com
- FAST.com
- Northern Light, nlsearch.com
- Google.com
- Excite.com
- Inktomi.com
- Go-Infoseek.com

You can also apply your knowledge base to the five big directories for generating more quality traffic:

- Yahoo.com
- LookSmart.com
- Lycos.com
- OpenDirectory.com
- Snap.com

With your new expanded list of keyword phrases, go back to your Web site. Expand and enhance your use of keywords in the body of your Web pages, in your page titles, your meta tags, and ALT attributes. With the list of keyword phrases you create using the Goto.com keyword database, there is no need to attempt to include every phrase on every page. Target certain phrases on certain pages of your site.

Periodically, review your Web site traffic reports to measure your success against your plan and to establish trends. Search for your site on the important search engines using your keyword phrases and record your position based on the phrases you are targeting. If your site is not the number one site for the keyword phrase you are evaluating, compare your HTML code to the Web page that is number one. Also, check to see if your site is listed in each of the top search engines and directories. Resubmit at any search engine or directory that has not listed your site in its database.

Applying the practice of keyword phrases will increase your ranking position and the amount of traffic to your Web site from search engines and directories, which will increase your overall business.

MAKE THE MOST OF YOUR META WORDS

Much has been written about the importance of peppering your site with meta words and meta tags (discussed in the next section) so that you earn high rankings in the search engines. Elaborate, comprehensive strategies have been devised. The combinations of words that you use on your site to describe it are important.

One of the easiest ways to draw up a list of potential meta words to use on your site is to visit the sites of your competitors. Once on an individual site, you can click on page source, and see all of the meta words and meta tags that your competitors use. While this is a reasonable strategy to get you started, you don't want to stop there. After all, if you only use what your competitors are using, how will you stand out?

You don't want to be exactly like everybody else; that is not marketing differentiation. When you are perceived as offering the same products or services as everyone else, you have to contend with vigorous price competition, and that's a losing game for entrepreneurs.

To draw up your own effective list of words, visit gainWeb traffic.com/keywordpnts.htm, which offers a variety of keyword suggestions.

Once you've assembled 15 or 20 keywords and phrases, visit well-known search engines such as Yahoo.com, Lycos.com, Excite.com, and AltaVista.com, and type in the keywords and phrases you've put together.

You will see which sites come up as a result of typing the words you wish to use. Now, add a few of them at a time, go back to the search engines, and over time (days, weeks, and, for some search engines, months) note how your standing in the rankings may be increasing.

Submitting your site to the various search engines takes time. Many have different sets of criteria and different sets of rules. Some want you to complete formal submission applications.

Don't make the mistake of overloading your site with unnecessary repetition. Some sites actually penalize you for such practices. Simply use the most appropriate words and expressions to convey and describe what you do, and emphasize these keywords at the top of your pages— as headers to new sections—and as sub-topics, and your rankings in the search engines will increase.

META TAGS MAKE A DIFFERENCE

Meta tags are the most efficient way to let search engines know what your site is all about. Using clear and concise meta tags can increase the chance that your site will obtain high rankings on the leading search engines.

Meta tags are hidden descriptions of a Web page. They describe the site's content so that search engines can more easily find what they are looking for. Meta tags are even more important for sites that contain frames or numerous graphics. They are used as a part of your HTML code, and by some search engines to index your page. Rather than letting the search engine take the first few words or paragraphs to use as your keywords, meta tags allow you to tell the engines what to use.

There are three types of meta tags. The first is the meta-tag keyword attribute. This is where you can enter your keywords using up to 1,000 characters. For this tag, be concise. Look at what actually appears on your page, and choose words that accurately describe it. The second type is the meta-tag description. This is where you write a description of what your site is about. Use several of your keywords in this description. Finally, there are ALT tags. These are used for any images that are contained on your page. The tag is a text description that will be displayed as the image loads. Visitors to your site will be less likely to become impatient and leave if they have an idea of what they are waiting for.

> *A*void misusing meta tags. The most popular tactic is to create meta tags with the most popularly searched terms, even though they have nothing to do with the Web site. Using this tactic, you might generate higher rankings. However, most of the visitors won't be interested in your site's content.

Many pornographic sites have used this trick by adding celebrity names to their meta-tags. However, search engine architects are becoming more aware of this tactic and are on the lookout for sites that misuse meta tags. If you are caught using unfair techniques, your site can be deleted from search engine rankings, costing you time and prospective customers.

Keep in mind that meta tags are used differently by every search engine. Some will give preference to sites with keywords in their meta tags, and some will not. Nevertheless, they are a means of controlling how your page is displayed by search engines. With proper and effective use, your meta tags can help interested people find your Web site easily and increase your business. It's a nice return for your marketing efforts.

THE BUG WITH A NICE BITE: VIRAL MARKETING

Increasing the return on your marketing efforts is what viral marketing is all about. Imagine a marketing tactic that combines speed, economy, and effectiveness into one, and comprises viral marketing at its best. Viral marketing could work for your business.

Hotmail used one of the first and most successful viral marketing campaigns. The small message contained at the bottom of each Hotmail user's e-mail tells other people about the service provided by Hotmail. Another example, Blue Mountain Arts, uses animated e-cards that bring recipients to the company Web site in order to access their animated card.

The key to viral marketing is to develop a network of existing customers to do the marketing work for you. Each customer who signs on to use Hotmail's free e-mail service spreads the "virus" and "infects" their own network of friends and acquaintances with Hotmail's message. The little tag at the bottom of the e-mails was so effective that it gained Hotmail 12 million users in the first 18 months.

People are much more likely to listen to the recommendation of a friend than to respond to a mass-market campaign. People tend to trust the opinions of their close friends and family. So viral marketing may not reach as many potential customers as a mass-market campaign, but the ones that it does reach are more likely to become customers.

Viral marketing depends on spreading a company's message through the network of its customers. The success of this system relies on the customers' belief that they are receiving something in return. The virus needs to be attached to something worthwhile that customers are willing to pass on. It has to be free and unimposing. People don't want to be responsible for involving their friends in a scheming marketing campaign. Overall, it has to be easy for customers to spread the message.

There are some drawbacks to viral marketing. If a company experiences an overwhelming response to a message, it might not be able to handle the increase in business in such a short period of time. Also, viral marketing has negative potential. If a campaign becomes too commercial and excessive, it might repel more customers than it attracts. The keys to successful viral marketing are balance and preparation.

Having successfully infiltrated the business-to-customer market, it is expected that viral marketing will become a presence in the business-to-business market. Clearly, for small Web-based businesses, viral marketing has great potential. In a world in which words travel as fast as one mouse click, the idea is simple and profitable. If you provide effective services or products, and offer a simple way for customers to spread your message to others in their network, you just might start a virus.

OFFLINE PROMOTION FOR YOUR SITE

Advertising offline is a way to initially connect with potential customers, and if done with precision, it can be a highly beneficial way to connect with the specific audience that you hope to attract to your site. Unless your site has incredible, broad-based appeal to people of all types, you are most likely trying to attract a certain type of individual with specific wants, needs, and interests. Realizing exactly who this target audience is will save you a lot of wasted time and money in advertising efforts.

Twenty years ago a company had to primarily advertise on the major network channels and in the major news publications. Today, there is a wealth of independent media with specific appeal in which advertising is available. For example, a Web-based company, Chapel HillRent.com, was established by a couple of college kids hoping to help other college kids find affordable rental properties in and around Chapel Hill, North Carolina.

Although it took time to establish the site, it was their offline advertising efforts that expanded the company and made it successful with thousands of visitors every week. The owners of Chapel HillRent.com realized that their strongest customer base was students in and around the University of North Carolina at Chapel Hill. They took their advertising efforts (and budget) directly to where that audience would see it best by advertising in the local food delivery service's publication, in the university's newspaper, and directly on the university campus.

When you understand your market, or at least who might be likely to buy your product, you can save your company significant money in advertising costs, and more importantly, increase your number of site visitors.

B y connecting with your customers in their world, you are more likely to attract them to your site than if you advertise to the larger, general public.

THE KEYS TO WEB PRODUCT SALES:
INVENTORY AND PRICING

According to *Time Digital*'s Bill Syken, if you sell products, two characteristics that are key to Internet marketing success are extensive inventory and competitive prices. You might be saying to yourself, "I don't have that much to offer," or "I'm only offering a specific service and not an actual product." Syken asserts that your site should ideally include both. Realistically, you might find that only one is applicable to your site. If that is the case, master that one quality.

Having an extensive inventory means many different things. An Internet site that has a decent-sized inventory and is extremely easy to navigate is more likely to do business than a site that has a huge inventory of products, but whose visitors cannot find their way around. If it's possible to expand your inventory and offer more products to your shoppers, then it is as important to make those products easily accessible.

When continually expanding the products you offer on your site, remain aware that customers do not want any hassles. They do not want to waste any more time looking for products on your site than necessary.

When expanding your inventory, if the primary product you offer strongly relates to other products that you could offer, but don't, then maybe you want to look to expand your inventory to include those other products. For example, DVD Express at dvdexpress.com is a site that offers a wide selection of DVD movies (as do many other sites). DVD Express, however, expanded its inventory to include movie posters and clothing with movie-studio logos. By doing so, DVD Express has set itself apart from its competitors by offering what they do not.

Say you sell high quality sleeping bags for the rugged outdoor person. You might find it beneficial to sell other products relating to that customer, like tents, backpacks, or other hiking gear. It may seem simplistic, but you would hate for a competitor's site to take your business simply because they offer everything your customer wants, whereas you only offer a few choices.

COMPETING FOR PRICE HAS ITS PLACE

If it's not feasible to expand your product inventory, or if you're offering a service rather than a product, then make sure your prices are competitive with the sites that have larger inventories. This is not to say that you have to make your products or services cheaper. If they aren't cheaper, then they need to be competitive. You want to be able to offer some kind of incentive for customers to visit and shop at your site instead of at a competitor's site.

There are many sites on which you can buy software and hardware for your computer. This market is highly competitive. To be successful, sites have to offer competitive prices. Cyberian Outpost, a company that offers competitively priced software and hardware, figured out a way to make their site, outpost.com, unique.

When you make a purchase, the site unobtrusively recommends other products related to the one you are purchasing or those in which you might be interested. Although it may not have the cheapest version of a product, it offers something that may encourage shoppers to use the site rather than a competitor's, setting Cyberian Outpost apart from the rest of the field.

THIRD PARTY MARKETING

MP3 technology, the highly publicized method of storing and sending compressed music files over the Internet, is obviously popular among music buffs and techies. Users download songs in MP3 format off of various Web sites and store them as files on their computers. These MP3 files can be played back as music over the computer or on hand-held devices used specifically for MP3 playback.

Robert Goldman used the growing popularity of MP3s to capitalize on a growing market. His company, GetMedia Inc., based in San Jose, California, created technology that allows a person to get on the Web and find out the titles of songs playing on the radio.

GetMedia.com uses a Java-based application that embeds in a radio station Web site and allows stations using the service to display and sell what they play on their Web site while they broadcast the music on the air. A listener can learn more information about the band, song, or CD on which the song is listed. GetMedia also allows users to backtrack through songs played on the radio station earlier that day.

The listener can choose to buy the individual songs as a CD from the radio station through GetMedia. The radio station sells music, which they already play for free to receive added revenue. The site handles the shipping of the CD and receives a percentage of the sales.

"You listen to the radio, and if you like what you hear, you're going to buy it," Goldman told *Inc.* magazine in the May 2000 issue.

GetMedia is more than a CD store. It relies on an established audience of radio station listeners and uses the popularity of radio stations as its marketing tool. Each station already has its own niche in the listening market and a Web site. The radio station is happy to let GetMedia on its site, because it derives a percentage of sales. In a crowded Internet marketplace, this strategy lets the company sell CDs without an expensive marketing campaign.

Goldman has managed to sign 35 stations and 2,200 more are waiting for their turn to use the technology. Goldman's marketing genius has established a Web presence by partnering with other companies—for mutual benefits.

> I s there something that your company can offer in return for an established Internet audience?

OFFLINE EFFORTS, ONLINE MARKETING EFFECTIVENESS

To wrap up this chapter, consider a seemingly small but important point. As a marketer, ask yourself which is more important: for you to proceed each morning based on your carefully crafted marketing strategy, or to proceed based on the e-mails in your in-basket?

When I come into my office in the morning, I take a offline look at the e-mails from previous days that I saved and arranged in various files and folders. Quietly and unhurriedly, I compose letters offline and put them into the drafts bin.

Since I have not logged on as the first activity in the morning and not allowed myself to be besieged by all types of new messages, I am in a far more commanding position to take action as I see fit and stay in control of my time and marketing efforts. To make this strategy work:

- *Have plenty of online file folders available.* Most communications software packages enable you to create as many file folders and subfiles as you choose.

- *Create a variety of folders on a temporary basis when an issue or project is at hand.* Then, eliminate the folder when the significance of the issue recedes or disappears. Because you can rename, combine, or submerge folders with the click of a mouse button, and because the nature of your work is probably dynamic, it makes sense to move folders in some way at least once a week.

- *Create a series of template responses.* Whenever you have to give an answer more than a few times, or disseminate a message to several recipients, use a prewritten response. You can always eliminate templates that are no longer useful.

- *Whenever you come across an interesting Web site address, but find you don't have time to visit it immediately, send yourself an e-mail containing the address.* Better yet, create a template with the subject line "interesting Web site addresses," and, as you gain each new address, go back to the template and re-save it and continue.

By any measure, e-mail is a wonderful means of rapid communication. By using simple techniques, it need not be the burden that so many entrepreneurs perceive it to be. At all times, remember this fundamental principle: you are in charge of your e-mail basket; it is not in charge of you.

3

BASICS TOOLS
FOR A
BOOMING MEDIUM

People read differently online than they do on paper, because most online reading is actually scanning. You have to learn how to write for users who scan. This includes using techniques such as keywords, subheadings, and bulleted lists.

One of the first keys to Web writing is cutting the fluff. People reading the text on your Web page want their questions answered quickly. Rather than using flashy vocabulary or elaborate sentence structure, stick to the basics when describing your products and services so that users won't lose interest and leave.

Organize your thoughts and your words. Your page needs to be a self-contained unit and have an introductory page that contains links to all other pages. Titles should be placed at the top of pages, so that they inform the reader about what comes next.

> The key to writing effectively for the online audience is for you to understand the medium.

ONLINE WRITING FOR ONLINE READERS

Relate to the audience. When a visitor is looking at a Web page, it is a one-on-one experience. Users will be more likely to fully explore your page if it relates to them. A good technique is to use the second person voice more often than you would in normal writing. This way, the customer feels like you are speaking directly to them rather than to a generic audience.

To learn how to write for a Web audience, visit the Web Developer's Virtual Library at www.wdvl.com and read Charlie Morris's essay "Writing for the Web." It provides an introduction to basic elements of style. You can learn how to beef up your writing while still keeping it tight.

To keep your audience interested, find the balance between credible tone and stuffy drone, important information and corporate doublespeak. It might be hard to ignore the writing habits that we have nurtured and developed since grade school, but even a slight adjustment to your writing techniques can make a big difference for your online audience.

BASIC CONTACT INFORMATION
FOR INQUIRING MINDS

People who visit your site want to know that you have a reputable, viable company behind your attractive screen. They want to know that they can get in touch with you in a variety of ways, without hassle. They want to know that they don't have to go hunting through page after page, screen after screen, to find the arcane link that finally leads to further contact information.

I t seems paradoxical that in the midst of the information revolution so many otherwise well-meaning Web site owners fail to offer fundamental information that they need to give site visitors—basic contact information: address, phone, fax, and e-mail.

In one study of more than a 100 sites, a survey team found that less than 10 percent provided their physical street addresses, towns, cities, zip codes, or phone and fax numbers for site visitors. What's worse, among those who did provide such information, it wasn't always easy to find. People had to go through several screens and use their thinking caps to figure out where such basic contact information might be located.

If you believe that you can exist in the hearts and minds of all site visitors only in cyber space, think again. Some people insist on knowing where you're located. They want to have alternative means for contacting you. This is particularly true if you sell any products over the Web. To presuppose that someone will be willing to fill out a registration form, complete credit card information, and simply zap it to some GU— geographically unidentified—entity is presuming too much.

Strive to have an e-mail link on every page so that site visitors don't have to go hunting for it. This gives them the opportunity to e-mail you the moment they have the urge. The e-mail address(es) that you provide need to be to actual people who will respond in a personal manner, answering questions in no more than a day or two. The response needs to at least include the person's name and a company employee's name, in order to make it as personal as possible.

Someplace else on your site, one that's extremely easy to find, you may wish to include names of department heads if you so choose, even e-mail addresses of specific individuals. It is fine to post info "@your domain.com," but that could leave some visitors cold. You're not trying to hide, are you?

Many small businesses provide a list of all their employees, including their job functions and e-mail addresses. By doing this, a customer can connect with a specific individual who can answer a specific question more personally and efficiently. These days, with your competitor a mouse click away, if you frustrate site visitors and make them wade endlessly through your pages in order to contact you, you are going to lose the majority of them.

One of the easiest strategies for posting your contact information is to simply create a long rectangular box that traverses the bottom of each page or many of your pages. Then, as visitors scroll down and see the first such box, and subsequently see it on other pages, the concern and mystery of where to find you physically, if they need to, immediately dissipates. Here's the contact information that I provide at the bottom of the majority of my Web pages:

Jeff Davidson, MBA, CMC • *"Helping people manage information and communication overload"* http://www.BreathingSpace.com © 2002
2417 Honeysuckle Road, Suite 2A • Chapel Hill, NC 27514 USA 919-932-1996 • Fax 919-932-9982 • Jeff@BreathingSpace.com

SOUND OFF?

Beyond the printed words and clever graphics, sound is a viable Web page tool, *when used properly*. Human beings are hard-wired so that we simultaneously process information on all sensory levels, whether or not we are conscious of doing so. In fact, studies have shown that we are better able to absorb, retain, and recall information when it is conveyed using multi-sensory methodologies. You can take advantage of this trait of the human mind by judiciously using sound files on your Web site.

Company officers or staff members can record messages for Web site visitors that can be played by clicking a link to the message. In the intangible world of the Web, the sound of a person's voice can go a long way toward making people feel good about visiting your site. Make sure anyone who records messages for your site is well-spoken, because messages that are mumbled, said too rapidly, conveyed flatly, or presented in a thick accent may alienate Web site visitors rather than welcome them. If no one in your firm fits the bill, consider hiring an actor or voice talent to record messages for you. Extended sales pitches are not what you're aiming for; keep these messages brief, both to shorten download time and to make sure you don't lose your visitors' interest.

Another way to use sound is to set links to make sounds when they are clicked. Different kinds of links can make different sounds. For instance, you could assign one sound to link the main section of the site; another sound could be associated with links to subsections within a section; and links to pictures and links to other pages could each have their own distinctive sounds.

You can employ sound starting at the beginning of a typical visit to your site by playing a quiet, tasteful soundtrack of background instrumental music. Alternatively, you can set certain pages to play background music, or you can program different pages on your site to play different soundtracks. Of course, not every site needs to play background music; a bowling ball manufacturer or an accounting firm probably wants to refrain from doing this, while a genre book retailer or a college student-oriented site might benefit from it.

Seek to use professionally recorded and distributed music, not music you create yourself using an HTML editor. Make sure you address copyright and songwriter royalty issues. (One way out of this situation is to use music that's in the public domain, such as many arrangements in classical music.)

The Web remains a mostly visual medium, despite the proliferation of applications and techniques for developing and enhancing Web sites. Sound files can differentiate your site from the rest of the Web, boosting user recognition and optimizing the overall experience of using your site.

PICTURES: STILL WORTH A THOUSAND WORDS

Got photographs? They are a necessity on your Web site. You need photographs of your business, your products, your employees, your equipment, and anything else that potentially gives a visitor a sense of you. When you click onto one of the major news media sites, such as CNN.com or NYTimes.com, you immediately expect to see a variety of new photos based on the lead stories of that day.

While no one expects the Web site of a smaller business to offer such a continual and changing variety of photos, visitors to your site maintain some expectations as to what a highly professional, credible site should include.

Give your customers what they expect, like photos and scans, as well as the usual array of visually appealing graphics. Hence, your goal as a small business entrepreneur is to constantly be on the lookout for photo opportunities. Anytime you interact with customers and a photo can be snapped, it should. If you attend a particular function, whether it is a lunch, an awards ceremony, or a board meeting, look for opportunities to have photographs taken of you, particularly with others.

You don't necessarily have to bring your own camera, since many such functions will have a photographer on site. If you are attending a meeting at a major hotel, particularly if you'll be saying a couple of words, chances are a photographer may be on site for the event, or the hotel or facility may employ one.

When is a better time to have a photo taken than when you are dressed up to the hilt, in a sparkling room, with showroom lighting, surrounded by vibrant people? Thereafter, find a way to put it on your Web site. Maybe it needs cropping. Maybe it needs to be lightened or it needs more contrast. With the variety of graphic enhancing software today, such as Adobe Photoshop, you can gleam the best from your photos in no more than a few minutes.

The same can be said for scanned items as well. Suppose you receive a letter from a highly satisfied client who sings your praises in glowing terms. Scan that letter in full color, so you can post it on the Web site (presumably with the permission of the writer). You might even devise a section devoted entirely to letters and other expressions of praise that you receive.

W hether a visitor to your site is there for the first time, or the tenth, well-placed photos help convey the image that you wish to achieve.

As an alternative to listing individual letters, you can also create a collage, if you are in a situation in which you receive letters of praise often. Likewise, if you generate excellent news coverage, you can post individually scanned articles and features, as well as create a collage of them. The collages can serve as site maps to the individual documents. Then, users simply have to click on a portion of the site map to have the scanned document appear in full.

IMAGE MAPS LURE VISITORS

Besides photographs, image maps can also be used to attract visitors to your Web site. An image map is a picture divided into regions that customers can click on to link to other pages on a Web site. The image itself can reflect and reinforce the marketing image you want to project.

An image map adds color and appeal to your site. It is especially useful when what you want to convey is expressed better in pictures than words. Say, for example, your company has multiple branches spanning several states. You might set up a map of the United States where your Web site visitors can click on their cities to link to a page describing a branch serving their areas.

Some people (right brain) relate to images better, while others (left brain) relate to text. Your image map might contain a set of rooms reflecting the structure of your site, which would appeal to visually-oriented individuals. An alternative set of text links would satisfy the left-brain contingent.

The downside in using image maps is that the large graphics typically used for these maps take a long time to load. In some cases, however, an image map may actually speed up your page if it replaces multiple icons, when each icon needs to be called up separately. In addition, image maps are more complex, and entail finding or creating the right graphics. Once you have the image, however, a software program can help you set up the hot spots: the coordinates on which your visitors click to link to other pages.

Two ways to handle the finished image include:

1. *The server side, in which it goes through a server.* This more traditional method sends the coordinates of hot spots on the map to a Web server, where a CGI (Common Gateway Interface) script interprets them, then tells the server what Web page to send back. The script is fairly standard, and your Internet service provider undoubtedly has one. Still, you'll have to coordinate your efforts with your provider, if you're using an outside ISP. The process of running the script will slow down access to your page a bit.

2. *The client side, in which the browser does all the work.* With this method, you set up the image map entirely on your own, as you would a GIF or other graphic on your page. This avoids the additional interaction with the Web server, resulting in a faster response or loading, and it's simpler to set up. However, though the major browsers recognize client side image maps, there still may be some browsers in use that do not.

APPLETS ATTRACT ADVANTAGEOUS ATTENTION

Java applets are small programs for generating a variety of multimedia effects in Web pages. With an applet you can shade text, scroll messages, bounce images, animate pictures, emit noises—everything from subtly sublime to garishly grandiose. Java programs, which run on a Web user's computer via the person's browser, also permit an expanded, more efficient interaction than what you can achieve with such tools as CGI scripts, which operate on the Web site's server.

The applets are written in Sun Microsystems' Java (files with a .java extension), a cross-platform programming language specifically designed for the Web environment. The Java files are then compiled into byte-code (files with a ".class" extension). The class files are what run an applet on a Web page, but applets only work with browsers that support them.

Applets vastly increase loading time on an average Internet user's computer screen. So use them judiciously and sparingly—to impart a particularly dynamic message that can't be achieved in another way.

To develop your own applets, you need to understand programming in general and Java in particular. Determine your goals. Like most of the more sophisticated Web page design tools, Java applets slow the loading time.

T he more complicated the effect, the longer it takes to appear. So use applets where they have a clear purpose. Then, decide what you need. What kind of an effect are you looking for? Shaded text, changing colors, animated images, or some other element?

One of the best-known sites to track down applets is Gamelan.com, which bills itself as "The Directory and Registry of Java Resources." Another good place is The Java Boutique. Here the applets, though not numerous, are easy to find, download, and use. Search for "java applet(s)" in the major online directories and search engines.

Download the appropriate applet(s). In some cases, one class file will do it. Other times, you'll need a package of class files, since some build on others. It's also important to handle the original source code file

(.java), which contains the program you can view in any text editor. Though you probably won't want to modify it, viewing it could clarify questions you might have about the particular applet and how it works.

USE ANIMATION INTELLIGENTLY TO HOLD ATTENTION

You don't have to be a techno whiz to make your site more attractive to your Web site's visitors. Animated GIFs please the eyes and hold the attention of your potential customers. An animated GIF works like a cartoon flip book or a section of movie film from which several related images, each with a progressively different position, are viewed in rapid succession. The advantage of this type of Web site animation is that it's easy: easy to build, easy to embed, and easy to access.

To construct your own animated GIF create a series of GIF89a images in a paint program such as PaintShop Pro or Adobe PhotoShop. Then use an animated GIF construction program to put the images together. GIF Construction Set, a program (costing $20) from Alchemy Mindworks that can be shared with other users, has a wizard that zips you through the construction process in a few minutes. You can then use the more advanced features to refine the GIF.

You can also use the program to wade through the whole process on your own. If you're using Microsoft's popular Web authoring program, FrontPage, you probably have a GIF animator that came with the program. For those who do not wish to do it themselves, sources of animated GIFs pepper the Web. *Yahoo!* lists numerous collections in its "animated GIFs" category.

Once you have the animated GIF, reference it in your HTML document like you would any other GIF. But, you may want to use a GIF animation program to limit the number of times the GIF repeats its animation cycle.

If users are at a page long enough, they'll want the animation to stop, because it soon turns from innovative to distracting. The movement can draw your Web site visitors' eyes away from the more important parts of the page. You may even want to set repetitions at only two or three.

Animated GIFs sport some appealing features. Depending on its size, an animated GIF can be up and running on screen fairly fast. People whose browsers don't support animated GIFs can still see something— they're not completely shut out of the process as they are with other animation tools, such as Java applets. For them, only a stationary image, which is the first frame of the animation set, will appear on screen.

SET YOUR SITES IN SITE MAPS

Your Web site can be carefully designed and user-friendly, but some visitors are still bound to be confounded when they are looking for particular information on your site. This is why the site map was introduced. The site map is usually a button you can click or menu item that visitors can readily find. Put it on your opening screen in a rather prominent position.

Site visitors know from visiting other sites on the Internet that the site map will give them a quick lineup of all of the features that your particular site offers. Then, presto. They can click on those features or items of information of particular interest.

It's frustrating coming to a site and looking for some particular feature only to be greeted by too many options, too many hyperlinks, too many places to turn. There are some sites that are entire worlds unto themselves containing so many elements and offering so many features that over-information junkies would appreciate them.

Regardless of the complexity of your site, the site map feature is the "port in the storm" that tells visitors that you have their best interests in mind. You want to make it easy for them to find what they need, and not take up a lot of time doing it.

Most site maps are offered in the form of an index alphabetical by topic, some with subtopics and subcategories. Each item listed is hyperlinked. Some sites go so far as to offer their own site search engines, allowing visitors to insert a word or group of words to help them quickly find exactly what they are looking for.

As with other Web features, you can use your site map, site index, or internal search engine as a marketing feature. Let visitors know through your site design, or other marketing literature and marketing campaign in which you engage, that these options are available.

If you're in a highly competitive field (and who isn't these days?), offering and promoting such helpful site tools may make the difference in procuring and securing new customers versus losing them to your competitors.

4

SITE INCLUSIONS FOR STRIKING CYBERGOLD

uiz time: what makes sales professionals feel warm all over? A qualified lead. Someone has directly asked you for information about your product or service, and you intend to fulfill that request as quickly as possible. If such a lead came to you via e-mail through your Web site, it might be one of thousands of requests you see each week. How do you respond to all of these potential customers promptly, without spending unreasonable amounts of time and money?

YOUR FRIEND, THE AUTO RESPONDER

Auto responders can do the job for you quickly, accurately, and automatically. They are computer programs that answer incoming e-mail messages (or messages submitted through a completed form on a Web site) by generating an automatic e-mail reply. For instance, your Web site could have an e-mail link allowing interested parties to send you a request for more information. An auto responder could reply to this request by returning a prewritten answer.

Auto responder replies usually arrive in the recipient's e-mailbox within minutes. Because they can reply to requests 24-hours, seven-days-a-week, auto responders can significantly enhance your lead contact capabilities.

> Businesses can tailor auto responders to fit their own needs. Your prospects might send an e-mail to one e-mail address, while customers send customer service requests to another. An auto responder will send the prewritten reply, which you choose in each case.

You may want to do follow-ups with your list of prospects. But do you have the time it takes for a well-timed, accurately targeted follow-up with your entire list? Auto responders can make that task much easier by generating automatic follow-ups for you. You may wish to send your leads follow-up marketing pieces that are different from the ones you send your customers. Auto responders can help with this task, too.

When a prospect buys something from you and becomes a customer, transfer that person from your leads list onto your customer list. Then you can keep sending mail to your leads without worrying about alienating your customers.

Other common auto responder features include the ability to make the response more personalized by inserting the prospect's name or other pertinent information into the reply message. Reply messages can also automatically be forwarded to another address or addresses. Auto responders make the chore of e-mail marketing an easy, productive task that puts time on your hands and money in your pocket.

A HIGH RETURN INTERNET MARKETING TECHNIQUE

In sales training you're often told to follow up, follow up, follow up. "That's great advice and it certainly works," says Web-marketing guru Tom Antion, "but it's quite a bit of work even if you have the best contact tracking database program. Someone still has to make the calls or send the faxes or e-mails, unless they use auto responders."

Auto responders now automate this process and allow you to multiply yourself thousands of times with a few keyboard strokes. Antion offers an example illustrating the importance of auto responders.

> Suppose you get the same question from customers over and over and you and your staff are spending too much time on the phone or sending e-mails back to the people asking the question. You'd set up an auto responder that has the answer to the question and publicize it to your customers.

Subscribers to Antion's electronic magazine at www.antion.com/ezinesuscriber.html know that they can send an e-mail to linktrade @antion.com and immediately receive a return e-mail giving them instructions on trading links with his Web site. Hence, he doesn't have to deal with these e-mails or do anything until someone actually puts up a link and requests that he reciprocate. This saves him an enormous amount of time.

A specific type of auto responder can serve as a proactive sales tool. "A sequential auto responder will follow up with additional responses for as long as you want," says Antion. "When a customer requests information the auto responder replies immediately as usual. Then, at intervals you set, the auto responder sends another sales message, and another and another until the prospective client 'buys or dies.'" Actually, they can click to stop the e-mails any time they want.

Several prospect contacts are usually required to make a sale and most people fail because they don't make the follow-ups. Now, this process can be automated.

Antion also offers a free seven-day mini-course on e-marketing. Nearly 1,200 people signed up for this free course the first day it was offered by sending an e-mail to minicourse@aWeber.com.

The course offering is still available. To gain a firsthand idea of how it works, send an e-mail to minicourse@aWeber.com or visit aWeber.com and sign up for your sequential auto responder.

Antion's auto responder dutifully sends registrants one piece of the course each day. He reports that he generated $6,885 in sales the first week from giving away a free course. Yet the auto responder costs $15 per month. You can contact Antion at tom@antion.com or antion.com. For more information on auto responders in general visit Autoresponders.com, a hub for information about e-mail auto responders, auto-responder service providers, and marketing-specific auto responders.

THE UNDERESTIMATED TIP-OF-THE-DAY

As simple as it sounds, many Web visitors appreciate sites that offer a "tip-of-the day" and visit them on a daily basis, often in the morning, to glean the day's tip. My own site, for example, BreathingSpace.com, offers a daily tip that changes automatically at midnight. In the course of one year, visitors are offered 365 tips, or for a leap year, 366. My tips are all related to the concept of having more breathing space in your life. On rare occasions when the system was malfunctioning, and the new tip wasn't offered, I actually received e-mails from several parties who alerted me about the situation.

Many sites offer philosophical tips, which assist readers in reflecting on various aspects of their lives. For example, sites that encourage positive thinking offer some daily message of optimism. Religious sites offer daily prayers. Literary sites offer quotes from famous authors.

Is offering a tip-of-the-day a major marketing strategy? In itself, not likely. Taken as part of the overall mix of what you include on your site, offering a tip-of-the-day can work well.

To start, you don't have to come up with 365 of them; instead work on one month's set of tips. Then, stay one month ahead. It helps to look at a calendar for the coming year so you can align your tips with the days of the week, holidays, and other special occasions. On Valentine's Day you could have a tip about love, on Mother's Day a tip about mothers, and near the first of September a tip about going back to school.

When you consume all 365 tips, feel free to dispense the same tips again for the coming year. Few Web site visitors, even those who visited your site every day to read the daily tip, will be aware or concerned that one year's set of tips was the same as the last.

It's likely that no one will know the difference. Even if someone does, the value of the tip a year later hasn't decreased. After all, in the course of the year, people's lives and circumstances change. Different issues arise. A tip read one year, versus the same tip read 365 days hence, would be viewed anew.

In subsequent years, however, it probably does make sense to develop new sets of tips. You can only run the same information for so long.

A s an added enhancement to your Web site, you can collect all the tips for the last week or ten days and offer
them to visitors, perhaps as a hyperlink from the current day's
tip. You could also offer a whole month's supply of tips, a sea-
son's, or if you are ambitious perhaps even the entire year's tips.

You could also assemble a month's, a quarter's, or a year's worth of
tips into alternative products such as one-a-day calendars or reflection
booklets either offered for free or as salable products. The simple addi-
tives to your site are what make your customers feel at home.

A NATURAL PROGRESSION: TIP-OF-THE-WEEK

Offering a tip-of-the-week on your Web site works much the same
way as offering a tip-of-the-day, with some notable variations. As you
can get away with a single phrase or sentence in offering a tip-of-the-day,
the tip-of-the-week invariably needs to be more substantial. Here, you
want to offer at least one paragraph, if not several.

At BreathingSpace.com, I offer a tip-of-the-week, which changes
on Sunday night. The tip-of-the-week is a full page of ideas, usually in
checklist or bulleted format. Thus, the reader is able to gain a major
idea, with several supporting ideas or action steps that comprise the
checklist.

After a tip has run for one week, it then goes into a second position
under the new week's tip, and after it has appeared there for a week it
goes into a third position. In other words, the current and previous
weeks' tips are all offered at the site so any given weekly tip appears for
a three-week viewing.

Visitors are also afforded the opportunity to receive tip-of-the-week sheets from months back upon request.

Each tip-of-the-week sheet has a title, my byline, my copyright notice, and the year. Obviously, you can't stop people from copying and pasting, printing, and otherwise extracting such tip sheets. Still, fixing the copyright notice affords some protection.

If the prospect of assembling 52 tip sheets seems onerous, take heart. Once again, you only need to be about a month ahead, thus you need four to five tips in the bag at any given time. Moreover, you don't have to have the full complement of 52 tips for 52 weeks. You could slide by with as few as 26, simply repeating the tips once a year. Again, few visitors are likely to notice or care.

> Even if people visit your site and see a tip they saw six months ago, they are still likely to view it with new eyes— it will have new meaning for them based on what challenges and issues they are currently facing.

You may quickly find that your tip-of-the-week is one of the strongest draws you have in inducing people to continuously return to your Web site. Once visitors find your tips to be credible, insightful, and useful, they will be more likely to bookmark your site and more likely to return on a regular basis.

VARIATIONS ON TIPS

Whether or not you have a weekly magazine, you still have the opportunity to present links to Web sites that you find to be highly useful to this select market. Suppose you serve a market of between 100 and 2,000 customers. You dutifully collected all of their e-mail addresses and can send a broadcast e-mail that includes the links to these sites to all of them.

Here's how it works. Let's say you're in a lumber supply business. Your market consists of 384 home centers, large hardware stores, and retail lumber supply yards. You are one of several wholesalers with whom your market does business. To keep your name at the forefront of their thinking, why not submit to them the link to one key Web site on a weekly basis that would be of strong interest to them?

You come across a forestry consultant who maintains a wonderful Web site on current developments in U.S. forests, long-term forecasts, reports on new chemicals, and other current information related to the quality and supply of lumber. So, as your first Web tip-of-the-week, send out a small paragraph to each of those customers in your database highlighting this site and including the actual link.

The following week, send out a small paragraph describing another site that offers superior lumber marketing techniques. The third week you find a site that talks about lumber preservation techniques for retail outlets. Week after week you send a simple paragraph and hyperlink to your valued customers. You don't inundate them. Enough of them will find many of the links that you submit to be worthwhile and actually follow through and visit the site. In fact, you may want to send the tips less frequently than every week, such as every two weeks or one each month.

Meanwhile, you are positioned as the conveyor of excellent information that enables them to more effectively operate their businesses. As a result of this continual small service you provide, you further establish and strengthen the bonds that you have with your customer base. They are more inclined to call you, more inclined to order, and more inclined to regard you as one of their favorites. This gives you a better excuse to call them when you need to, and you might be greeted more cheerfully when you do.

If the prospect of finding some key Web site to send each week seems daunting to you, fear not. You can assign the most junior staff person to go to the various Web search engines, and, using key words, such as lumber, lumber supply, forest, forestry, lumber shipments, and lumber preservation generate a qualified list of sites. In other words, you can virtually automate the process.

> W hy not have at least four or five sites stored away at any given time, and leap weeks ahead? Thus, you can go at least a month without having to make any new searches and still have your Web site tip-of-the-week feature functioning smoothly.

ANOTHER VARIATION: NEWS TIP-OF-THE-WEEK

A related technique to the tip-of-the-week involves submitting a news tip-of-the-week to your established target market. Instead of searching for key Web sites that you know will be of interest to your target market, focus your search on news independent of the site on which it was found.

If you find it to be more convenient, again assign your junior associate to log on to the various search engines available. Some of those recommended include GoTo.com, NLSearch.com, Google.com, Hot Bot.com, AltaVista.com, and AskJeeves.com. Periodically have this associate type in key phrases related to lumber, maintaining the example discussed before to generate a list of hits.

Request that the associate then visit the sites to see which ones contain the gems. Then, he or she can simply extract relevant paragraphs and passages being sure to maintain the source information.

> With minimum editing, you can then create a weekly, biweekly, or monthly ad hoc magazine or newsletter that represents nothing more than your compendium of the number of news items you deem to be appropriate.

Given that you carefully choose the tidbits for inclusion and that you do a masterful editing job, your targets are likely to be appreciative. After all, you are giving them information that is relevant to their success or is of other interest to them. You have also saved them time, because they're not likely to have the time and energy to do this for themselves.

Once more you've established your company as the purveyor of not only the primary goods and services that you are in business to deliver, but also cutting edge industry information that would otherwise be missed by those who stand to benefit.

VISITORS LOVE ARTICLES

Posting articles on your Web site is a time-proven technique for generating repeat visitors. The articles can vary in length, from around 250 to 3,000 words. You can offer a single article or a series of articles. They can be permanently posted, rotated, or offered for a limited duration. These articles can be offered to any visitor via password, for a fee or as part of a club. Post them by topic areas, dates, titles, word lengths, or any other criteria.

Be sure to proofread articles thoroughly before putting them on your Web site. The most appropriate and effective articles for you to post are those that position you as an expert in your industry or occupa-tion. While it is understandable that an article of 1,000 or 1,500 words may have a typo or two in it, they detract from the professionalism of your site and could leave visitors with the wrong impression.

> In many respects articles tell site visitors much more about your services or capabilities than any other feature on your site, such as a résumé, listing of credentials, listing of clients, or descriptive background.

An article conveys your expertise to readers sentence after sentence. It's hard to say nothing in a 1,000-word article. If a supervisor in an engi-neering firm, for example, writes an article on reinforcing bridge sup-ports, a public notice has been made that they and the firm, are experts in this area. Someone requiring a subcontractor on a bridge design project may call the writer's organization merely on the basis of the article.

The fact that you can intelligently discuss a topic for that length or longer and offer relevant information, keen insights, and possible solu-tions to pressing issues to readers speaks volumes about your capabilities and expertise in helping clients or customers in your chosen field.

A posted article can lead to an invitation to speak before a particu-lar group. Every article can be made into a speech, and vice versa. Giving speeches will put you in touch with others interested in your subject area who will help broaden your web of connections.

TOLL-FREE NUMBERS GET THE NOD

You spend a lot of time and effort designing your Web site, honing and refining it so that customers will easily find it and use it. Now go a step further, and make it easy for them to reach you by phone. Does your company have a toll-free number? All of the 800 and 888 numbers are taken. The 877 series is nearly gone and undoubtedly will give way to yet another series.

From a marketing standpoint, regardless of the designated toll-free exchange, you can't afford not to have a toll-free phone number posted on your Web site. The cost of incoming calls has never been lower, and in most locations with most vendors it is under 15 cents per minute and in some cases far below that. Thus, even an extended call on the order of six minutes still costs less than a dollar.

> For the opportunity to have a live, interested party call you and verbally interact with you in real time, toll-free numbers are one of the world's best bargains.

Many customers still need assurance from somebody over the phone before doing business with an entity that they first found on the Web. Who can blame them? The Web is not a totally safe and secure arena of commerce. As a result, companies do go out of business, messages are transmitted incorrectly, and sometimes "stuff" happens that scares consumers.

Beyond giving customers opportunities to call, the mere posting of a toll-free number provides a measure of assurance. That number along with other items you include on your Web site add up to customers making a decision to do business with you over other sites. If you already have a toll-free number, and/or you have already posted it on your Web site, make sure it is prominently displayed. Posting your toll-free number on every page would not be over doing it!

There was little disruption in Web and communications capability following the World Trade Center attacks because nearly all systems had been completely backed at remote locations— a bit of wisdom the small business Internet marketers should heed.

HIGHLIGHTING FOLLOW-UPS AND CUSTOMER TESTIMONIALS

When potential shoppers arrive at your site, it is important to make them feel like valued individuals. You want to let them know they are not merely numbers. This can be done in several ways, and in turn will make all customers' shopping experiences positive ones—ones that they will share with friends and that will make them want to return to your site for other purchases.

Giving the customers a compelling reason to make initial purchases and then making them feel important even after they purchase are equally important. This may seem unnecessary—if they've already made purchases, you have obviously impressed them in some way. Yet following up with customers can help you in the long-run and make their experiences more positive.

One way to follow up is to send your customers an e-mail (or even call them) several weeks after they receive your product to ask what they think of it. You might ask them for a testimonial or for answers to a short survey that you can post on your site for other customers to see, in addition to your sales pitch. Many times, it will be another customer's feedback that will persuade a potential customer, and not the sales pitch.

Another key marketing strategy is to do "Testimonial Updates," in which you ask old testimonial providers to update them several months later.

B y keeping in touch with your customers you are building a relationship with them, building their trust in your company, and making them feel better about doing further business with you. You are gaining more valuable information about your customers as well, and what they need and want. In turn, this information will help you decide how to better serve your customers.

You also are giving your potential customers more than another sales pitch. You are making purchases more personal by associating the product with actual people who have bought it, were pleased, and would recommend it to others. If you think about it, there isn't anything to lose.

VISITOR COUNTERS MEAN REVEALING NUMBERS

One other neat addition to your site is a visitor counter. Many sites will display a visitor counter telling you exactly how many people visit each week, each month, each year, or some other unit of time.

It's not easy to know how accurate the visitor counter is, since many people will pad the numbers to make it look like their site is more popular than it really is. Still, when you visit a site with such a counter, it's interesting to note that substantial numbers of others have visited. Why is this so? Everybody loves a winner, and if a site becomes popular, others want to know.

BRING 'EM IN WITH BOOKLISTS

Much of what you find on Web sites is time-sensitive or updated on a daily or weekly basis. Other sites post information for the long run. For example, my site includes both dynamic and static information. One feature is called "Book Digest," where nearly 100 books are summarized. Visitors may download a book digest selection of their choice for free. I add to the book digest periodically, but basically it is a static portion of my Web site. Why not make your list dynamic?

Clients and customers are always looking for the latest and greatest information that will help them solve a problem, add to their storehouse of knowledge, or simply help them understand the problem better. Vibrant sites not only make old customers want to return, but they also draw in new customers. To keep your site vibrant, offer a list of recommended books and, in particular, book reviews. Such a list can be part of a magazine that you offer on a periodic basis or can be simply posted on your site.

M any people find booklists to be intriguing.

Think about the last time you opened up the *New York Times* and saw the bestseller's list. Could you avoid looking at the feature? Or could you do so when you opened up the Thursday lifestyle section of *USA Today* and saw its top 50 list? People notice booklists, whether the books are on bestseller lists, or recommended reading, or simply "Uncle Joe's Favorites."

My own list of favorite books, particularly in relation to dealing with change and flourishing in the cyber age include the following:

- *Managing at the Speed of Change* by Darryl Conner
- *Managing in Turbulent Times* by Dr. Peter Drucker

- *Technotrends* by Dan Burrus
- *Breathing Space* by Jeff Davidson
- *Becoming Digital* by Dr. Nicholas Negroponte
- *The Complete Idiot's Guide to Managing Stress* by Jeff Davidson
- *The Acorn Principle* by Jim Cathcart

Were you able to resist reading that list? Lists are appealing. You could go as far as Amazon Books.com does, as to posting your recommended reading list right on your opening page. The fact that you maintain a recommended booklist is also excellent fodder for promoting other aspects of your Web site. You can send out targeted e-mails, use postcards, and make references to your booklist on your company's letterhead.

How do you generate a list of books quickly and easily? It's not hard these days. You can go to Amazon.com, Barnes&Noble.com, or any one of a number of other online bookstores and quickly generate a list of current, popular books in your field. Also, you can peruse the bibliographies of books you currently own.

You can receive recommendations from clients and friends, and also ideas from the publications to which you subscribe. Your list does not need to include anything more than the title, author, publisher, and year—more than enough for readers to find the title if they want to pursue things further.

What about doing book reviews? This takes a little more time and a little more energy, but also can be a great service for your constituents. Your book review doesn't need to be more than a paragraph long, 100 words or less. Often, you can do a synopsis based on a longer review that you encountered in the *New York Times'* book review, the *New York Review of Books*, or your own local paper's Sunday book review section. There are also scads of book review services on the Internet, and the aforementioned online bookstores also have a bevy of reader comments from which you can prepare your own synopsis.

A t all times, maintaining a booklist, and going a step further by offering mini-book reviews, continues to help you position yourself as an expert in your field. You are knowledgeable, you are highly experienced, and heck, you are even well-read.

EXTENDING YOUR BOOKLIST

Art Burg, a speaker and trainer from Highlands, Utah has developed some innovative ideas in relation to recommended books on his Web site. Burg says that he added a section to his site that has received a lot of positive feedback from visitors, and provides additional revenue without the burden of inventory.

As with many Web site owners, Burg maintains a recommended book area. But rather than simply having a single list, he has divvied up the list into many sections. One section, for example, is entitled, "You'll Never Be the Same" books. These include many of the books he has read throughout his own life, either when growing up or as an adult. Each of these books is hyperlinked so that readers can order them from a certain online book vendor. The vendor then supplies Burg with a percentage of the profits for having sent in the referral buyer.

Another section in Burg's recommended booklist is called, "Books on My Shelf." These include books that he has also personally read over the years and that he finds outstanding and noteworthy, but are not necessarily in the same category as "You'll Never Be the Same" type of books.

Still another section on Burg's recommended booklist is called, "Books in My Bag." These include books that Burg is currently reading or at least has on the night-stand, and will eventually read. These could be books that his clients or associates have told him about, that he has gotten wind of by the Web, or simply picked up the last time he visited a book store. Unlike the first two categories, "Books in My Bag" changes on a continual basis.

A fourth area of recommended books is called, "Books of My Friends." These include books which visitors to Burg's Web site recommended. To encourage visitors to make recommendations, Burg has initiated a novel awards system. Each month he has a drawing from the names of those who made book recommendations. Announcing the awards system and the winner on the site, he then sends the lucky participant a copy of each of the books in his "You'll Never Be the Same" section.

> Whether you use a recommended booklist section or some other comparable feature, you can generate greater interest and participation among your Web site visitors.

Can you stratify your lists? Can you give rewards to visitors for participation? Can you encourage visitors in some simple but effective way to continue to contribute to your collection? Remember, the feature doesn't have to be with books. It could be with photos, new items, product recommendations, reviews, songs, sounds, or even opinions. Once your feature gains momentum, you will have a bevy of regular Web site visitors who check back on a periodic basis to see what is new and recommended, and all the while, you will be the beneficiary.

...AND NOW FOR RECOMMENDED MAGAZINES

Developing and publishing a magazine roster is similar to the concept of publishing a booklist and book reviews. The roster could include magazines, journals, or periodicals of great interest to your visitors. You can use many directories to scout for those magazines that would make your list. *Bacon's Magazine Directory*, published in Chicago, offers background information on more than 12,000 periodicals in the United States.

For each publication site, full address information, phone, fax, e-mail, and a Web listing are provided. Also, department editors, circulation, and a description of editorial content are provided. No matter how specialized your products or services, or how arcane your industry, you will find at least 12 to 20 publications listed in *Bacon's*. Call 800-621-0561.

Other good reference sources for scouting magazines worth presenting to your site visitors include *Hudson's Newsletter Directory*, which is a compendium of newsletters, in this case, highly professional and mainstream, circulated (often for a fee) on a regular basis: weekly, monthly, quarterly, and so on.

Magazines for libraries, *Standard Rate and Data*, and *Working Press of the Nation* also have voluminous lists of magazines, journals, and periodicals worth considering. All of these reference materials are available in the reference section of any city or academic library.

As always, you don't have to necessarily own any of these volumes; send an employee to the library to copy the key pages.

To provide an even higher level of customer service, in addition to listing the publications and offering a synopsis of what is included in each, you may also wish to hyperlink them so that visitors can quickly follow up on their own if they so choose.

50 Periodicals Worth a Periodic Perusal

Advertising Age	Men's Health
American Demographics	Millionaire
American Spectator	Modern Maturity
Apartment Living	Money
Architectural Digest	Mother Jones
Atlantic Monthly	The Nation
Better Homes & Gardens	National Review
Boardroom Personal	Nations Business
Business 2.0	The New Republic
Business Travel	PC World
Civilization	Psychology Today
Common Cause	Red Herring
Conde Naste Traveler	Responsive Community
Consumer Reports	Robb Report
The Economist	Selling Power
Entrepreneur	Southern Living
Esquire	Success
Forbes	Technology Review
Fortune	Town & Country
The Futurist	U.S. News & World Report
George	Variety
Harper's	Vital Speeches of the Day
Kiplinger's	Wired
Ladies Home Journal	Worth
Marie Claire	Yahoo Internet Life

FREE DOWNLOADS AND FREE SAMPLES

It's ironic to say that giving away your product can increase both consumer demand and your sales, but that's exactly what many Web sites (both new and successfully established) do.

> Offering potential customers a free sample, or free downloads, of the product gives the customer a taste of what the full product can give them.

The initial cost of giving away free samples of your product may be greater than the return, however. The potential for a substantial increase in profits is expanded, at least more than if no sample were offered. The theory behind free samples is simple. By exposing people to the product, you can encourage them to be paying customers. A terrific example of a site that has made this method work for them is RealPlayer.com.

Started simply as a site that offered its customers a way to play audio and video online, RealPlayer.com has expanded significantly to become one of the leading audio and video players used on the Internet. It now offers players that allow the customer to listen to over 2,500 radio stations online, download audio and video faster, burn customized CDs, play video games online, plus much more.

Possibly the most influential reason for its rapid growth is that RealPlayer.com has always offered a free downloadable version of its basic player. Nothing fancy or complex, this basic player allows the customer a sample of what the advanced player can offer. By allowing the customer to try the product, RealPlayer.com has given the client a reason to need its product. How does this happen?

RealPlayer.com offers the free sample, and though it may seem like a good player at first, the customer will soon find that downloads could be faster, that they might be able to listen to more radio stations, watch more and better videos, listen to longer audio clips, and so on if only they were to upgrade to a more advanced product. RealPlayer.com offers a product that costs $39.95.

By offering the free sample, however, RealPlayer.com found out who its consumer is (by way of a short form before the free download), made its name known to the customer by offering a worthwhile free version of its software, and created the potential for the customer to want/need the product.

> Offering free samples or downloads online, when show-rooms and the actual products are unavailable for the customer to experience, could be the determining factor between whether someone purchases your product or your competitor's.

USING SELF-REPORTED INFORMATION TO THE BEST ADVANTAGE

You've already visited several Web sites that offer the registration-type pages that induce visitors to fill out their complete addresses and contact information. Why would any visitor want to take the time to complete such a form? Because there is some major direct benefit for doing so. The benefit might include having a question answered, receiving a free item, being privy to survey results, and so on.

Registration forms routinely ask visitors to offer their first name, last name, street address, town, state or province, zip code, country, e-mail address, and often their phone and fax numbers. Other questions you may wish to include are:

- Where did you hear of this site?
- How can this site be improved?
- What features would you like to see?
- Which features did you like most?
- Which features did you like least?
- What would make the site more valuable for you?

One of the best ways to induce people to fill out self-reported registration pages on your site is to offer them some free information that automatically is sent to them once they have completed the form. This could be a report, a tip sheet, a chapter from a book, a pass code, or anything that site visitor is likely to deem of value.

The information you collect from visitors who take the time to fill out your registration page can be quite valuable. They can give you new ideas for marketing your site, product service offerings, and how to reach others in the target niche.

At all times, be up-front and honest with these special visitors. Let them know about your privacy policy and exactly how you intend to use their data. Never abuse your relationships with these visitors.

Don't inundate registrants with too-frequent messages about you, your site, your products or services, new promotions, or special deals. They can only handle so much, and they might be encountering too much already from other sites.

Make it exceedingly easy for them to give you data, by using drop down boxes from which the visitors can select one or several options that require no more than a mouse click. Let them use the tab key to move in either direction between data fields. This gives them a sense of maneuverability and control that they don't otherwise enjoy when they are forced to proceed in one direction with limited options.

WHAT'S YOUR BEEF?: COMPLAINT OR GRIEVANCE FORMS

Your natural inclination may be to resist posting a feature that enables visitors to air their complaints, but read on. The wisest and most successful entrepreneurs know that ignoring problems, not allowing customers to have a forum for airing grievances, and not being aware of problem situations in their businesses are extremely costly from a marketing standpoint.

An old axiom says a disgruntled customer tells at least 26 other people. Whether or not that's accurate, the sad reality is that unless you give people the opportunity to air their grievances, you may never have a chance to hear about them. The customer simply withdraws. In the cyber age, this has never been more true, because your competitors are only a couple of mouse clicks away. Offering visitors the opportunity to air their grievances by some special feature or hyperlink on your site provides two valuable types of marketing intelligence for you:

1. It gives you the specifics of the situation so that you can rectify things for that customer and potentially win them over in a way that engenders even more loyalty.

2. It alerts you to a problem area that may impact many of your customers and gives you the opportunity to head off the problem before it hurts your revenues.

You may not enjoy reading about what your company has done wrong or how you have let down a particular customer, but it is far more palatable to find out about such issues early than to find out about them too late.

Your ability to address individual issues, word for word, head on, shows that customer and all such customers that your company does care. This can make a big difference in both retaining that customer and marketing to them for the long-term.

Sure, you'll encounter an irate visitor or two who simply likes to complain. Or you will receive long diatribes that aren't necessarily focused or clearly related to your products and services. Read them anyway for the minor gems they may contain.

If you notice a trend among grievance letter writers, that certainly presents strong evidence toward changes you may need to make to improve your overall service. But don't wait for lots of complaints before making a change. Even one well-crafted letter from one single customer may be all the information you need to institute swift, effective change.

From a marketing standpoint, unless you are privy to the specific grievances of customers, you have little chance of retaining their business. A grievance unaired is a grievance that lingers.

A grievance aired and resolved is the formula for a long-term relationship with your customer.

LET THEM EAT QUIZZES

Pop quizzes in school probably made you shudder. Quizzes on the Internet, however, particularly self-scoring quizzes, take on a whole different meaning for your site visitors. Most people who bother to take them at all regard them as somewhat fun. A self-scoring quiz gives the user the opportunity to gain instant feedback, the most desirable and quite necessary feature if you decide to offer a quiz. A quiz is a strong marketing inducement to your site because people always want to gain more information about themselves.

At Dr. Tony Alessandra's site, Alessandra.com, you can link over to his alternative site PlatinumRule.com and take a self-scoring quiz that tells you which of four personality types you are most closely aligned with. Dr. Alessandra's quizzes, and good quizzes in general, share some of the same characteristics:

- They take only a few minutes, at most, to complete.
- The quiz-taker is spared laborious typing; answers can be chosen with drop-down menus, or by merely clicking one of several options.
- The quiz questions are short, easy to read, and easy to understand.
- The quiz form itself is rather simple in construction and easy to navigate.
- Few instructions or directions are needed; the user can quickly get started.
- Upon completion with one click, the quiz-taker receives their result. The result may be in the form of a paragraph explanation, a score, a category, or some other easily understood form.

Dr. Alessandra's quizzes are designed so you can take them over and over again. By answering certain questions a different way, you would end up with a different result. Many sites on the Internet that include quizzes also give you the opportunity to conveniently alert a friend who may wish to take the quiz. My site offers four quizzes, each self-scoring, with each giving you the correct answer if you happen to miss it.

Such quizzes make for excellent marketing tools, because many newspapers, columns, articles, and magazines like to tout quizzes on the Internet once they hear of them. So, when you design your quiz, as with all other site features, make sure that the word gets out. Let people know about your quick and easy, fun-filled quiz and many of them will find the time to take it.

As with posting articles on your Web site, tip sheets, or other types of useful and reliable information, posting a quiz positions you as an expert in your field.

Your ability to design, score, and interpret the quiz-takers results indicates that you are an expert in this field and someone who the user can reasonably count on for related products and/or services.

SURVEYS SAY A LOT

Every marketer, both on and off the Web, asks, "What does the customer want?" Well, here's one easy way for Web marketers to find out. Web site user surveys can give you the exact information you're looking for with virtually no effort or cost on your part.

Many prominent Web sites frequently use customer surveys. Webzine *Salon.com* uses a Java subroutine to make a separate survey window open when randomly selected users first access *Salon*'s main page. Users are given the option to participate in the survey. If they don't want to participate, they can close the window and go on to view the main page. *Salon* encourages survey responses by offering respondents free goodies or chances to win larger prizes.

Set up your survey by installing a link to the survey on your main page. The link could say something like, "Click here to take our customer survey and gain a chance to win a free vacation to New York!" When users click on the link, they are taken to the survey page.

Questions on Web surveys can be quite similar to the ones you'd ask in person or through the mail. Obviously, you want to know your visitors' demographic information and buying habits. Most important for Web marketing is to ask questions about your users' online behavior. What Web sites do they regularly visit? This will tell you where to target your marketing efforts.

From which Web sites do they regularly purchase items? Go to those Web sites to learn how they're attracting your visitors' business. How much time do your visitors usually spend per online purchase? This information will guide your own pricing and business planning.

Regular customer interactions over the Web offer a golden opportunity to solicit opinions. How many times have you run into a snag while trying to buy something in a store or over the phone, and wished you could give the company feedback right away? The Web provides the perfect medium for gathering that kind of information. On every page of your site, give customers a link they can use to send you e-mail.

The text for the link needs to specify that customers can use it to make complaints or communicate problems to you. That way, users can immediately tell you what the problem is, while it's still fresh in their minds. The customer has gotten something off his or her chest, and you've gained a valuable opportunity to make the customer happier.

DON'T OVERLOOK CHAT ROOMS

Chatting, as you know, is a form of real-time communication in which the keyboard is used to type messages that are instantaneously shared with other people in the online chat room. Since chat rooms have gained a reputation as cyberhangouts for kids, they are frequently overlooked as a medium for online networking.

More businesses are discovering that installing chat rooms on their sites can be an excellent way to gain exposure.

To take advantage of chat rooms, you can add one to your business's Web page. You can download them for free from sites like www.quickchat.org and multicity.com. Before adding chat to your Web page, consider how much traffic your site usually receives. Chat will be beneficial only if you have enough people interested in using the service. The whole concept depends on a community of interested people, so individuals will stop trying to use it if there is never anyone there.

Chat rooms can be used in many different ways. You can host your own discussion on the topic of your choice, namely your product or services. While you are hosting, you will be able to choose the direction of the discussion and hopefully entice some new clients. You can chat about new products, customer support, or even have your company president chat with your customers. You can also participate in a chat as a guest. In other words, you can go to a chat that someone else is hosting and network while learning for free.

Chat rooms can also be used to conduct client meetings. You can set up an appointment and meet to discuss business issues. Staff meetings can also take place in a chat room, especially if your business or company employs a number of telecommuters.

Teaching an online course is another great use for a chat room that can bring potential business. You can set up a time and a topic and then pass the word to interested parties. During the class, you can answer questions and offer help to the "students." This technique can stimulate business and keep your customers happy.

The people that you attract to your Web site have a common interest in what your business has to offer. A chat can be an exciting tool for gaining and sharing knowledge while allowing potential clients to become more familiar with you and your business.

FORUMS FOR THE FORTHRIGHT

Forums are a Web-based communication method that can promote your business and encourage your customers to remain loyal. A forum functions like a newsgroup. Messages, which are stored on the Web site, are written by members of the community and can be responded to by other members of the community. While chatting is a real-time activity, messages on forums can be read and responded to at any time.

Usually there is a slight delay between when a guest posts a message and when it appears on the forum for others to see and respond. The delayed timing facilitates some in-depth discussions more readily than a chat community.

Forums often are divided into subject areas so that people who use them can easily find their areas of interest. An outdoor-gear store might use a forum to create categories for different activities such as camping, backpacking, swimming, fishing, and hiking.

Another example is the Lipton Kitchens Food Forum that has a section for recipe recommendations, one for new ways to cook with Lipton secrets, and one for general cooking tips. Whatever your business or service area, you can devise categories to promote a better sense of community among the forum users.

Forums readily help with marketing and promote your products and services. You can derive a special forum topic that relates to your business's products or services. Customers can then post questions, which you will answer and post for everyone to see. You can increase your credibility and give helpful advice about your business when you establish a forum.

Another type of forum that may be helpful to your business is a job board. Job boards used to be the Web version of the newspaper classified ads, but they are quickly becoming much more. Along with online recruiting sites, job boards are changing the way employers hire people and the way employees find jobs. On a job board users can assess their skills, build their résumés, research companies, and chat with others doing similar things.

There are also sections providing information for employers, such as skills testing and background and credit checks. They function as an entire human resource department. Almost the entire hiring process can be done over the computer since résumés can be forwarded instantaneously to employers.

5

WEB SITE DESIGN
FOR THE SUBLIME

hen Adam Morgan of Broken Arrow, Oklahoma decided to put his six-person landscape-design firm on the Web, he didn't know anything about designing a successful Web page. Now, with a successful site that brings in new clients to his firm, Morgan still doesn't know anything about Web design. Morgan followed a simple rule—when you don't know how to do it yourself, ask for help.

Of course, Morgan had choices about how to get his Web page up and running. He settled on Quickbooks, an accounting software program that cost him a little more than $100 and included access to a simple site-builder.

Morgan filled out a three-page form, including essential information about his company, and the program searched the Web for a domain name. In 24 hours the site was established and in a few weeks his firm was seeing positive results in several new clients.

Basically, Morgan's site serves as an aggrandized business card for the firm, much less technical than what many small business entrepreneurs are looking to set up. His story, however, illustrates an important lesson. If you don't know what you're doing on the Web, seek help.

GET HELP DESIGNING YOUR SITE

Many small business owners and entrepreneurs want to establish online businesses. Hosting companies often cater to this need, offering a basic package deal including catalog-like design and credit card processing. What if your needs are more specialized?

Alex Algard, cofounder of a car-stereo store SoundDomain.com, invested in help designing a comprehensive and specialized site catered to the business. Algard hired a programmer to design a comparison shopping mechanism for the site. He realized that customers are more satisfied making expensive purchases such as car stereos when they know how the products compare to one another.

SoundDomain.com also includes detailed information to inform shoppers about car-stereo technology. Algard invested in help designing an online glossary that helps shoppers understand the terminology pertaining to their purchasing decisions. The results on Sound Domain.com have proven the effort and investment worthwhile. The site attracts millions of page-views per month and the company keeps customers satisfied.

> The decision to go online doesn't require you to learn all the technical aspects of the Internet and Web design.

Don't be afraid to invest in help with the design and upkeep of your Web site; then you can successfully execute your e-commerce goals.

TINKER ALL THE WAY

If it's not already apparent, one of the success factors of Internet giants such as eBay and Amazon is that they evolve on a predictable basis. eBay.com has accommodated sellers by offering better photograph hosting services. eBay also changed its policy for posting feedback on buyers and sellers so that both parties are better protected.

Constant tinkering is the key to the success of many "household" name Web sites.

Beyond that, eBay added new trading categories such as products for small businesses and larger ticket items such as automobiles. Hence, the broad swath of buyers and would-be buyers who visit the site saw that eBay.com was not simply a highly viable trading post for people to find one another throughout the world. It also proved itself to be a dynamic, user-responsive, ever-developing exchange forum, and information center for users, novice to veteran.

Amazon, ever the ambitious giant on the Internet, continually adds features such as the ability for friends to share purchasing lists with one another, and a variety of discovery tools for finding available merchandise. The selections themselves, such as wireless phones, tools for business and personal use, and a variety of consumer electronics, all but ensure that its existing customer base keeps returning. Customers understand how the Amazon ordering system works, so why not continue down the path of least resistance?

When Amazon added the *Independent Seller* programs, the *Z-shops*, and its own auction component the company drew both high praise and criticism. The Author's Guild complained that by offering used books on its site, Amazon was diminishing the sales of newly published books and thus reducing authors' and publishers' potential income. Weathering the criticism, but retaining the features, the company's long-term quest toward profitability continued.

> Constant tinkering helped both Amazon and eBay keep increasing revenues while other e-commerce sites flopped. The lesson for the small business Internet marketer is that continued site enhancement is both a prudent and expected aspect of offering products and services online.

Give your customers something new to look forward to. Not every change will be warmly embraced. When you make changes that aren't well received, you'll hear about them quickly enough. Fortunately, you have the power to re-change whatever prior changes you've made that haven't gone down as well as you might have hoped. The Internet is dynamic, and your site needs to develop an element of dynamism as well.

INCREASING WEB DESIGN EFFICIENCY

An effective Web site loads quickly and allows visitors to navigate efficiently and easily. The golden rule of Web site navigation is the two-click rule. Anything a visitor wants to see on your Web site needs to be available within two clicks of the home or start page.

Navigating a Web site is difficult without a simple, clear table of contents and clear page headings. Visitors need to know where they are, where they can go, and how they can return to where they came from. If visitors hit a dead-end or want to turn around, they will quickly exit the site if there is no easy way back to the home page. With a table of contents in the margin, they can proceed directly to another page on the site.

JCrew.com provides its users with simple navigation and easy movement between sections of the online catalog. Wherever a visitor is on the site, the table of contents can quickly take them to another heading or return them to the home page.

Another easily navigable Web site, StoneWalrus.com, allows its customers to browse by choosing a region, product category, or animal type. Using one of these categories, customers are almost guaranteed the ability to find their desired product.

Web sites can further ease the viewing process by constructing a personalized site for each visitor. The IBM homepage asks customers to categorize their browsing interests as "Small Business Options," "Personal Computer Options," or others.

The site then takes the visitors to a page constructed to cater to their interests and needs. This not only gives the customers a greater sense of identity with the company, which now seems genuinely interested in their needs, it also allows them to navigate the Web site more easily.

> If visitors are pleased with the design and layout of a Web site they are more likely to stay and make purchases. As a small business online, it behooves you to design your Web site for efficient navigation, so that increased sales are only a few clicks away.

USE YOUR TIME WISELY AND GET HELP

Ty Boyd, a Charlotte-based executive speech trainer and professional keynote speaker offers these astute remarks about marketing on the Web. "It has taken me a long time to learn this simple lesson: As an alternative to spending all your time learning to drive a truck in order to move something from one place to another, you usually hire a good truck and driver to handle your job.

"Likewise, when you want to market on the ever-changing Web, and you already have your hands full, spend your limited time finding the best professional in the business to become your sword. That person will grow your business while growing their own. And you can keep doing the things you do best to build the demand for your Web marketed product or service."

This same basic theory motivated Timothy Fong to found LassoBucks.com, an online work-exchange cooperative. Fong realized that many people who do freelance work or are launching new businesses have excessive amounts of free time. This is time that could be better spent working and earning money. So he created an online clearinghouse for time.

Users log on to the system and make an offer—they describe their skill or service, the quantity available, the cost per unit, the start time, and the expiration date. The offer is posted on a trading circle, organized by location and interest, and other members can make bids on the offer.

When someone accepts, your account is credited with the appropriate number of LassoBucks, minus a 5 percent transaction fee. Your currency allows you to buy services from others that can help you grow your business.

"Time is precious... Those who can extract value from their excess time will make a huge impact on their business," says Fong.

Maybe your small business has something to offer to others, in return for help with the challenges of marketing on the Web. Bettering your existing skills might be more useful for your business than trying to master the online frontier. Consider the benefits of such an exchange for yourself.

"You have heard it said many times in your life: *You do what you do best, hire the best to do for you what you don't do well. Both will profit.* And you will be way ahead of *the game*. I have done that (finally) in our business, with great results. The secret is not in learning how to build a clock, but to use the clock for the advantage it has to offer. Caveat: Attempting to shorten the process of selecting the right expert can cause grief....to your peril."

Take Ty Boyd's advice. Find help for the tasks you can't handle alone. Everyone, including yourself, will profit from the effort.

GIVE VISITORS THE INFORMATION THEY WANT

As you design your site, consider the interests of customers and visitors, and don't skimp on content. For a small business site, interesting and informative pages will bring new visitors to the site, and keep bringing old ones back. Depending on your business goals and the needs of your customers, each site needs to have the appropriate amount of content. With the right attention to content, a Web site can serve visitors well by acting as a resource for information in a particular field.

Focus on constructing a clearly designed site by offering information that can help, or simply entertain, visitors. If visitors find the site to be an effective source for information, they will reward you with their

The world is full of information, flying at us from all directions at a high speed. An effective Web site shields visitors from a confusing design and avoids barraging them with too much information.

patronage. John Shelley found this when he launched his company's site about five years ago.

Shelley is the owner of Shelley's Garden Center & Nursery Inc., in Felton, Pennsylvania, a nursery with about 15 employees. He enjoys keeping up with his online customer community by updating his Web site almost daily.

Shelley launched the site with a base investment of about $1,500. The comprehensive site includes weather reports, news features, a gardening newsletter, and a virtual tour of the nursery. Shelley also includes daily tips and occasionally writes a weekly column.

With a large customer following built up, Shelley believes that customers keep coming back to the site because of its reliable, informative content. He thinks that they experience a good feeling of the business from the site, so they feel comfortable doing business with the nursery. What seems most valuable in Shelley's case is his willingness to provide what customers want to know.

Be willing to redesign and consider new or different information that might benefit visitors to your Web site. If aspects of the site go unnoticed, they might be unnecessary. Along with filtering new information, a good Web site edits out the old. Cut anything that seems unnecessary and always update and add more when it seems appropriate. Hereafter, continually consider what information concerns your customers and apply those findings to your content.

W ith effort, your site can become an asset to your customers and your business.

BRING ON THE NEW

Never underestimate the visitor's appetite for the new. Popular news sites such as CNN.com, USAToday.com, and WSJ.com, thrive on hourly updates of breaking news stories. Even sites that change only once a day or once a week have an advantage over their more staid competitors.

Some people check in every day for the latest Dilbert offering. Many visitors report visiting simple sites that offer a thought-of-the-day, quote-for-the-day, tip-of-the-day, or list-for-the-day. Some people, and I don't know why, are enamored by cool site-of-the-day features. This day in history is popular among Web surfers.

SIMPLICITY PAYS

The power and simplicity of Google.com is a clear illustration that screen clutter is neither necessary nor desirable to attract a broad swath of Internet users. Loading up your site with bells and whistles may make some visitors feel comfortable and others uncomfortable. In the main, however, people want tangible benefits. Quickly receiving accurate information has to be near the top of the tangible benefit list.

Anything that diminishes the users' ability to obtain desired information, such as having to click through several screens, read excessive directions, endure whatever you think is cute, fancy, or otherwise a vital embellishment to your site, is a misallocation of your time and efforts.

Google.com quietly but majestically has surpassed Yahoo.com, Lycos.com, Excite.com, and the brunt of other cram-it-in-your-face search engine sites. There is a lesson for small business Internet marketers everywhere. Simplicity can work!

LOCAL SIMPLICITY

Rick Edler sells real estate in Los Angeles. When the Internet began to grow popular, he decided to put up a simple Web site to advertise his services. After some success with that site, he noticed that many Web sites were much fancier, with sound files, animation, and elaborate graphics. Edler wanted to put up a new site with a little more kick.

Edler's first site cost him $285, but he paid a Web developer $7,000 to put up his newer, more elaborate site. "We were going to dazzle everyone with all the technology, all the flash," said Edler in a February 2000 issue of *Inc.* magazine. The new site was colorful and full of wildly spinning graphics.

Edler was disappointed to discover that his new, fancy Web site was not generating much traffic. In addition, many of the viewers were not enticed to stay at the Web site once they got there. The problem? The new site, with all of its graphics and animations, took too long to load. Once it was loaded, all of the things happening on the screen were too busy; they tended to be distracting.

"So much was happening. You stared at it like you were watching a commercial. We were scaring people away," Edler said. For all of his investment, the newer, more expensive site was doing a worse job than the simpler, $285 site.

Edler decided that it was time for the new site to go. He spent another $2,000 to build a third Web site at edlergroup.com. The new

> When you are building your Web site, remember the time-tested principle: bigger is not always better. Internet users are a fickle, impatient crowd, and your site has to be simple and easy to navigate.

site was simple. Fewer graphics and animation made a quick loading site which encouraged visitors to stay.

Graphics and animation are great "bandwidth eaters"—they take a long time to load in the user's computer and make your Web site performance slow. Don't slow down the user. People do not want to sit around waiting for the information they want because someone has put up a lot of useless graphics. Also, remember that many of your customers may not have access to faster modems and computers.

> The Yahoo! Web site, at yahoo.com, is a fine example of using simple graphics to keep download wait-time to a minimum and make the interface simple for the user. Excessive bells and whistles can be distracting to the user. Web page viewers want a site that is attractive, but also easy to use.

DESIGNED FOR TRUSTWORTHINESS

Some consumers see the Web as chaotic. Although trust generally develops over time, your job is to communicate trustworthiness as soon as visitors make their first call on your site. Your goal is to appear and be trustworthy in your efficiency, design, and concern for customers.

How can you build trust over the Internet? Consistency and concern appear to be the keys. Customer needs are consistent and often predictable—they want something fast and easy. Many customers who arrive at a Web site know what they want. They simply want to determine if, and how, you can offer it to them. If you can't, then you're not worth their time and a single click will take them somewhere worthy of their patronage.

Ideally, a customer wants to access a Web site and move through its pages quickly, instead of spending time waiting for them to load. They want products to be organized and categorized so that they can easily find what they're looking for. According to interviews conducted with some Internet shoppers, they want to be able to go to a home page, use a search function to find their product, choose it, and check out.

An example of this speed and direct access is Clinique.com. Knowing that some customers already have their purchases in mind, they provide an express shopping feature that allows them to bypass the site index to a page with links to every item sold online.

Some Web sites allow for easier access to products by listing them under multiple headings. This makes selecting the right products simpler and faster. Instead of determining whether a particular dress qualifies as "What's Hot" or "Formal Wear," the shopper can find it under both headings.

Providing customers with fast, convenient service will keep them coming back. After all, if you're making the buying process difficult, then there might be something you're trying to cover up, which won't build a

M any online shoppers regard a Web site loaded with gimmicks and twists as a means of deflecting their attention from the actual products at hand.

sense of trustworthiness in your site. Shoppers like sites that are quick, obvious, and simple.

FROM SHOPPING TO DROPPING OUT

This leads us to ponder the important question: Why do people abandon online transactions, when they took so much time and energy to:

- find the site,
- decide to order a product or service, and
- begin the process of completing the online order form?

The following reasons showed up based on a survey by small office.com:

- 41 percent thought the Web page was too slow.
- 20 percent said the Web page looked unprofessional.
- 16 percent realized the site didn't take credit cards or the credit card that they had.
- 14 percent couldn't find the checkout area.
- 12 percent couldn't find a return policy.

What about Web site visitors who simply do not purchase a product online? A survey conducted by MyInfo Interactive reveals the top three reasons why consumers, who have not yet conducted a transaction over the Internet, would likely do so in the future.

1. Their privacy was assured.
2. The site offered significantly large price discounts.
3. They could return the item purchased online in the event of their dissatisfaction to a brick-and-mortar store.

These are all challenges that you can overcome.

1. For a privacy policy, emulate those that you see on other reputable sites.

2. While it's hard for small businesses to sustain a price war, you can certainly offer a competitive discount by visiting a shopper comparison site to see what others are offering. Then, if the numbers work for you, go ahead and offer the discount.

3. Having a physical location where items can be returned by dissatisfied shoppers may represent a challenge if you don't maintain a brick-and-mortar storefront. To compensate for the lack of physical location, obtain an Internet site certification, such as that granted by TRUSTe.org and BBBOnline.org.

PROVIDE CUSTOMERS WITH TRUSTe

As a merchant, it is important to collect information on customers, using polls, surveys, or questionnaires, in order to provide them with the best services possible. Customers, however, need to be informed of the purpose of your inquiries, so that they can feel more comfortable providing you with the information.

Building customer trust is mandatory as a Web-based merchant and there are many tactics that can ensure safety for your customers. Perhaps the most effective action, and one that's reassuring to consumers, is to use the TRUSTe privacy seal program.

TRUSTe, which stands for Trusted Universal Standards in Electronic Transactions, is based in Cupertino, California. The TRUSTe organization is a nonprofit, third party, overseeing service that helps businesses alleviate customers' privacy concerns, while also meeting their own needs.

For a reasonable yearly licensing fee, based upon yearly revenue, a Web store can reassure its customers by providing the TRUSTe privacy seal on its Web site. For Web consumers, this seal assures them that the company takes privacy seriously and will handle any personal information in a responsible manner. As a merchant, this means that more customers will feel safe and secure using your Web site to purchase products and services, which means more sales for you.

To obtain a TRUSTe seal, a Web site has to adhere to the specified privacy principles. Among these, companies need to inform customers of what kind of personal information they are collecting, how they use it, and if it will be shared, and the site must include information on how it obtains and updates visitor information. Also, the company has to provide customers with the option to block the sale or transfer of its personal information. Information on TRUSTe can be found at truste.org.

Merchants can also go to the site to receive help constructing their own privacy statements. The TRUSTe Privacy Statement Wizard can be found at truste.org/wizard. Having a privacy statement on your Web site is the most fundamental step toward providing safe, secure service to your customers.

A similar privacy seal service is BBBOnLine, a subsidiary of the Council of Better Business Bureaus, based in Arlington, Virginia. Like the TRUSTe seal, the BBBOnLine speaks to customers' privacy needs.

Privacy seal programs give your customers reassurance. They tell your customers that you are a trustworthy member of the online business community.

HIT THEM QUICK WITH YOUR GREAT OFFERS

Uri Evan started his online grocery business, Netgrocer.com, in 1997 with the idea to create a Web site that would sell groceries, but also build a brand image that would stick with consumers. The site, net-grocer.com, was initially designed to take users to a home page describing the company's mission and background before they could purchase groceries.

Netgrocer.com, however, was not doing well with the Web site. They were attracting many people to the site initially, but viewers were leaving before they even got the chance to buy. Sales were not good. Evan decided to ask Fred Horowitz, one of the investors in the venture, to help. Horowitz had experience in retail and could see that the Netgrocer.com site was trying too hard to create an image instead of selling products.

"Freddy placed more of an emphasis on retail and merchandising than the original team, which was more computer and system oriented," Evan said in a February 2000 *Inc.* magazine article.

Horowitz scrapped the design of the Web site that forced viewers to view pages of information about the company mission before they could buy groceries. He believed that Netgrocer.com was not doing enough to place the products in front of the users. Horowitz implemented a redesign that was more similar to a traditional retail approach—the new site has many pictures of products and coupon offers.

"Every supermarket can hang 20 or 30 posters near the entrance to provide information about the deals they're offering. That kind of merchandising was missing from our original site," said Evan. The site is now generating much more revenue and many more viewers are staying around long enough to buy something.

Having a brand loyalty does not matter as much on the Web, where users can quickly and easily click away to another site. Netgrocer.com was using some of the most valuable spaces in their Web site—the front pages—to build brand image. This valuable Web real-estate instead could have been used to focus on customers' interests and allow them to do what they wanted to do—in this case, buy groceries.

> Customers need to know what you can do and how you do it. Hit them quick and hard. The more time it takes for a customer to understand and access your services, the more likely they are to move on to another site entirely.

Are you willing to risk having your customers become impatient and leave? Merchandise your products up front, spoon feed 'em, and win.

DON'T GET CAUGHT UP IN TRAFFIC

Many Web sites point to how many individual page-views they get a day as an indication of how popular they are. Popularity, especially for the small business, does not always equal profit. Make sure that your Web site is attractive, but that it also generates a profitable business.

Erik Stuebe runs Blue Marlin, a company that sells vintage baseball caps. After meeting with a Web developer, Stuebe decided that a company Web site could increase his sales significantly—so he paid $35,000 to launch a site. The site, bluemarlincorp.com, was constructed beautifully, with eye-pleasing graphics and a huge amount of information about the history of baseball. You could also purchase Blue Marlin hats in parts of the site. Stuebe figured that the more people that came to the site, the more people would buy hats online. The site became quite popular and it was generating many page views a day.

Still, it wasn't selling a great deal of hats. Stuebe continued to put money into the budget for the site, but customers apparently were happier to buy their hats at a real store. The Web site only accounted for a tiny fraction of sales.

"Ninety-five percent of the people who visit the site don't purchase anything. Maybe they're more inclined to buy it retail," said Stuebe in a February 2000 *Inc.* magazine article. The site continues to be popular, but Stuebe has since decided to divert some of the Web site budget into other, more profitable areas of his business.

Many companies build Web sites with the ultimate goal of seeing how many visitors they can drive to it. For some larger companies, focusing more on increasing their name recognition, this is a useful business model. Small business owners have to be concerned with revenues—are users enticed to buy once they arrive at the Web site?

Are visitors buying products or seeing information that will be useful to them when they are considering your goods and services? Is the Web site merely a place they like to visit or are they using it and helping your business grow?

Before spending big money to build a site and promote it, make sure that the money invested will generate some return. Don't become carried away by thinking that making your site popular will result in mountains of cash. Inducing as many people as possible to view the Web site is important. However, attracting viewers is not enough. Your Web site has to add to the bottom line.

MAKE YOUR WEB DESIGN WORK FOR YOU

The following basic Web design principles will help you create your own site or work effectively with someone who creates one for you:

- *Make the site consistent.* Determine a design that best portrays the image you want to project and repeat the basic elements of the design on each page of the site.

- *Keep the design uncluttered for easy access and understanding.* Put links to all major sections, including the home (or opening) page, on each page of the site for easy user navigation. Give full contact information: phone, fax, address, and e-mail. People like to have a choice of response mechanisms.

- *Use graphics judiciously and sparingly.* Most of your visitors will have a standard dial-up connection to the Internet, at a speed that will almost grind to a halt when downloading numerous or large, complex graphics. Include graphics only to prove a point, illustrate a concept, or create a feel that's best done graphically. Pictures of construction sites for a construction company, for example, would be appropriate, because, in this case, graphical presentation shows what you do better than descriptive text.

    One construction company, for example, uses a digital camera to photograph its construction sites. The photos, which appear on its site, reveal the scale, quality, and appearance of the projects the company works on. In addition, the company uses a particularly attention-grabbing design on its testimonial letters page. The letters are graphically laid out on the page, as they might be on a small tabletop. Above this layout, quotes from each letter rotate on the screen using a simple technique: an animated GIF (a file format for Web graphics).

- *Refresh the site with periodic updates.* See what others are doing for ideas on what to add and what directions to take.

MAKE YOUR SITE SPEEDY FOR VISITORS

Putting someone on hold on the telephone for too long can cause the caller to hang up. The same thing will happen if you force a customer or client to navigate a confusing voice mail structure. Yet many business people make the virtual equivalent of these two errors on their Web sites. They build modem-clogging, graphic-laden pages, they make their visitors wait...and wait...and leave. Or, they create navigational structures that are inconsistent and nonintuitive; they make their visitors click...and click...and leave.

> Your visitor is a click away from leaving. Many Web surfers still use a 28.8 modem. Whether you build your site yourself, or hire an expert to do it, your choice is simple: eliminate speed bumps or eliminate visitors. Focus on providing worthwhile content, clean, fast-loading pages, and easy navigation, and your Web site will ring up business for you.

The following are some ideas to keep the customers from leaving your site.

- *Use fewer images.* If they don't provide information or draw the eye to something you want your visitors to see, the graphics aren't paying their way.

- *Use smaller images.* An image half the height and half the width will be one-fourth the area and one-fourth the file size, and thus will load in one-fourth the time.

- *Reuse images.* When a Web browser retrieves and displays a file, it stores the file both in memory (RAM cache) and storage (disk cache). Then the next time the same image is requested, it loads almost instantly. By using the same version of a logo on every page, rather than different versions, or the same icon several times on a page instead several different icons, you'll cut loading time significantly.

- *Optimize images.* Image editing software such as Adobe PhotoShop, PaintShop Pro, or the Image Composer program that comes with Microsoft's FrontPage Web-authoring program, can reduce the file size of a graphic by as much as 87 percent without reducing its size on the screen.

- *Link to sections.* Your home page needs to include links to all the sections of your site. Make it easy for your visitors to know what you have to offer and how to find it.

- *Link home.* Put a link back to your home page on every page. Make it easy for your visitors to reorient themselves if they're not sure where to go next.

- *Position links.* Put the links in the same position on every page. Familiarity breeds comfort. By the time they visit a second or third page in your site it should feel like home.

How else can you cater to your site visitors' need for speed? Here are some suggestions:

- Work on your Web site's load time so that the opening page appears within ten seconds even for visitors with slow modems.

- Allow true click and point capabilities for visitors who want to send an e-mail message to you. Don't make them fill out laborious forms, which will eliminate the bulk of the correspondence you receive.

- Let them click on your e-mail address so they can compose their e-mail and send it with the same ease and speed they do any other e-mail.

- Keep honing your site to increase visitor-friendly mobility. This means having easy road signs and lots of return options. Let people move around the site the way they want to not the way that you want to.

Finally, offer true links to what you do, not simply winding paths that you created to force them through a series of screens before they arrive at what they want.

6

TANGO WITH
YOUR CUSTOMER

I t could be said that there are two equally challenging tasks in using the Internet to market your business: attracting customers to your site and keeping them interested. Keeping customers on your site and returning to it increases the odds that you can hold their attention long enough to get your message across or sell your product.

FUN MIGHT BE THE ANSWER

Depending on what your business offers, free online games, various surveys, and amusing polls might be the key to attracting visitors. When using these slight additions to your site, it's important to learn what you can about the visitor rather than simply amuse them.

Online polls can give you this two-fold opportunity. Even if the daily poll you post on your site is arbitrary to your product, it engages customers to act on your site and gives them the chance to see how others answered.

P osting a poll on your site every day, you can learn more about your visitors.

Unlike a customer survey that provides you with basic factual information about your customers, a poll (if monitored closely) can reveal an attitude, opinion, or persuasion that the customer would not reveal otherwise. Such information helps you determine who your customer is, how they think, and possibly how they shop online. In turn, this allows you to better realize how to cater to customers' wants and needs.

SiteLaunch.com offers visitors free downloads of games, guest books, bulletin board software, etc. It also offers business owners a for-fee daily online poll that can be added to their sites. These polls may be general or they can be customized to the owner's wants. By having this feature, a site owner can ask specific opinion-based questions to customers in order to gather information, all under the guise of an amusing game.

REMINDER SERVICES

Here's a strategy with a different twist: A large percentage of Internet users live in a high-paced world of computers, pagers, cell phones, and increasingly efficient ways of accomplishing things in less time. With this trend of better, faster products comes a growth in the number of people who need help remembering all of the little activities that so easily become lost in the rush of life.

Lifeminders.com has a relatively simple idea. Lifeminders.com offers a reminder service that sends e-mails to people reminding them of everything from buying daily vitamins, to a friend's birthday, to an important anniversary or event, to the release of a new music album.

Customers first complete a short survey to become a registered member of Lifeminders.com. They are then immediately sent to a longer, more specific survey. The information gained in this survey customizes the kinds of e-mails they receive.

After entering important dates and other personal reminders the customer wants sent, each customer is asked to check other areas of interest. Lifeminders.com uses this information to send promotional offers and other general reminders customized to individuals' interests and needs.

With this service, the owners of Lifeminders.com learn important information about their customers and gain the potential to substantially increase their overall profitability. Lifeminders.com can now target that customer with more specific offers and promotions, avoiding the label of junk mail.

You may be thinking, "If my Web site has nothing to do with making promotional offers or announcements of a variety of products, how can a reminder service be of use to me?" The content of your site doesn't matter; the addition of a reminder service does several things besides those previously mentioned.

- It creates a relationship between your site and the customers, because they rely on your site for certain personal reminders.
- It allows you an alternative method to advertise your product (see viral marketing).
- It brands your Web site. After seeing or hearing a site's name 20 times, the customer will remember the name, the products it offers, and all positive attributes you assign to your site.

In short, while your site may have nothing to do with the kind of products Lifeminders.com offers, adding a reminder service to your site is a relatively small task that carries the potential for great reward.

TIME SENSITIVE OFFERS CREATE ARTIFICIAL URGENCY

It's amazing to see how compelled people can become to buy products when the time to purchase is limited. To make this work, contact a list of customers who have shopped on your site before. This list might consist of only a select group of people, or it may be everyone who has ever shopped on your site. Let each customer know that the offer is being made to only highly valued customers.

Then make a special offer and present it only to the select group, even telling them that the offer truly is limited. Note: Do not include this offer on your Web site where anyone may stumble onto it.

Perhaps the offer is a special discount or price, a "buy one, get one free" offer, or a "free product with a regular purchase" offer. Regardless, the offer must be incentive enough for the customers to feel compelled to take you up on it. Put yourself in their position. What kind of offer would oblige you to make a sudden purchase?

With the first notification of this special offer give the customers a redeemable coupon that they can use when they make the purchase. For example, give them a special coupon code that they can enter to redeem the offer. Also, in the first e-mail, give them the option to not receive any more offers or e-mails, and in turn respect this request. Some people are annoyed by unsolicited mail.

Last, make the offer time sensitive. In other words, set the expiration date of the offer to be soon (maybe four days) and stick to it. No one wants to feel as if they were scammed into thinking something that was not true. On the other hand, customers may take your next offer more seriously and act upon it. Also, follow up with the customer. Notify them once more before the offer is over. Be careful, though, because too many reminders could become annoying.

Assembling a package, making a deadline, offering a redeemable electronic coupon, and following up until the deadline have little chance of hurting your business in any way, but they do have a great chance of increasing your sales and visitor traffic.

OFFER A RUNNING TOTAL

If you offer goods via your Web site, regardless of what type of shopping system you devise, you have a primary role to honor. You need to ensure that you give the customer the opportunity to receive a running total at any moment with a single mouse click. Customers want and need to know how much is in their shopping carts, and they have to be able to do this with the greatest of ease. Otherwise, they may become uneasy.

Studies show that when customers begin to fill shopping carts online, they are much more inclined to abandon their purchases than through any other ordering mechanism, such as ordering by catalog, over the telephone, via fax, or in a retail store. It is all too easy to abandon an online purchase. Also, some customers are only testing the waters to see how the shopping mechanism works. As you learned in the last chapter, abandoning shopping cart purchases happens all too frequently on the Web.

For those who have an inkling to buy from you, however, you want to make the experiences as painless as possible. This means giving the customers the opportunity to not only see their running totals, but also to change the number of items in their orders, to delete items as they will, substitute items, and so forth. This level of ease and flexibility for customers bolsters your overall marketing efforts, because the net result is that more of them will stick with the order that they are building up and actually check out.

If you are unsure about how convenient it is, or you haven't run through the mechanics lately, right now is as good a time as any to visit your own site and start to shop as if you are a customer. Also, have friends and relatives visit as well and report back to you as to what they liked and didn't like, what worked and what didn't work.

You want to make sure the kinks are smoothed out, so that the visitor, who doesn't know you and has never met you, places a large order on the first visit, and then comes back for more.

SOCK 'EM WITH SALE SEARCH FUNCTIONS

Many successful Web stores include search functions that allow shoppers to search items throughout the site. Adding this feature allows consumers to easily locate the products they want and need, rather than going through endless links and indexes of products. Search features can add much to a Web site, making navigation easy and allowing click-through buying, but many sites fail to maximize the potential of this feature.

The key to providing customers with a good search function is to anticipate their needs. Some Web stores allow customers to customize their searches, narrowing the field to a particular price range. Amazon.com allows customers to search for items on the entire site or specialize the search to book or music sections. Acknowledging that different customers will have various needs gives the company the chance to predict the necessary design of the search function.

Jeffery Triggs' Web site, Global Language Resources, at global-language.com, provides an online modern library including nearly 600 literature classics. This former Rutgers English professor, who also helped develop the prototype for the Oxford English Dictionary Online, included a customized search engine on the GLR site. Anticipating the needs of academics, college students, librarians, and literary lovers, Triggs constructed a search engine that allows them to locate and access the large volume of texts on his site.

Beyond customizing the search function for products, Web sites can also include search functions for other databases on the site. For example, a small regional chain with a Web site might allow customers to search the nearest retail outlet.

> Keeping customers' needs in mind, search functions can increase the user-friendly nature of a Web site.

CALLING ALL ADS: ALLOW FREE CLASSIFIED ADS

Allowing customers to post free classified ads can be a reliable traffic-booster for your Web site. Increased traffic isn't the only benefit classified ads can offer; they'll also create consumer goodwill, develop user loyalty, and foster a sense of community among visitors to your site.

Some of the Web's most successful sites have prospered with the use of free classified ads. Yahoo! (yahoo.com) is a prominent example.

Classified ads are only one of the many free services Yahoo! offers its users. Netscape (netscape.com), vying with Yahoo.com to be a premier Internet portal site, also offers classified ads as part of an array of complimentary services for users. These ad services are used by thousands of visitors every single day for everything from employment searches to dating.

You don't have to be an Internet portal site to use classified ads. If your users have some sort of common concern, you can count on that common denominator to provide the raw material for a successful classified ad service.

If you're a paint retailer, for instance, you can set up a classified ad service that helps professionals in the industry find firms that are hiring. Noncompeting companies could buy and sell new and used equipment through your site. You could even allow users to post auction notices in your classifieds.

The benefits of classified ads aren't limited to retailers, either. Other kinds of Web sites have used free classified ads successfully for years now, including sites on spirituality, such as grandmother-spider.com, and magazines, like the erotica site nerve.com. Sites put up by distributors, entrepreneurial service providers, and hobbyists all have provided fertile ground for free classified ads.

To enhance the usefulness and appeal of your classified ads, allow as broad a spectrum of ad types as you can without being absurd or inappropriate. For example, a software development company obviously has no business running a dating ad service, but an ad category allowing role-playing gamers to make connections might be much appreciated by many of the typical visitors to a software company's site.

Organization is of primary importance to a well-functioning classified service. Make sure all ads are readable; make sure they're all in the correct classifications; and don't forget to delete them after a specified period of time. Handled correctly, a free classified ad service can give Web users one more reason to spend time on your site—and to spend money with you.

FULFILL ORDERS, MAKE MONEY

With online sales come processing and shipping. For small businesses on the Web, the challenge is to offer products and services and then deliver with success. The job isn't done until a satisfactory delivery is made. When things run well, customers' needs are fulfilled and they are likely to return again.

There are many options for small business shipping and handling, but not all options are necessarily feasible for you. Not every company is large enough to have its own shipping and customer-service divisions and not every company can afford to out-source its shipping and handling needs. To best manage shipping services, companies need to evaluate their needs and resources.

Here is a wrinkle you may not have considered. Outsourcing shipping and handling is probably the most attractive of all options, allowing you to focus your energies into other areas of your business. Many companies can handle these tasks for you, and they often offer a wide range of services for your business. The best way to find one is to ask around. The important thing when choosing a particular company is to make sure that it's willing to work with your company and its needs.

You can offer easily trackable shipping and delivery information. Once someone makes a purchase from your site using your online shopping cart you can link directly with the shipping and tracking systems of major express delivery carriers such as UPS, FedEx, and DHL. After selecting your favorite carrier, place a clickable button on your site that enables customers to track their packages. Label the button *track my package* or *package tracking*.

> When customers can automatically see their latest tracking information, this provides assurance, cuts down on questions you have to field, and increases the probability that customers will do business with you in the future.

You have to choose a shipping company to distribute your goods. Once you open an account with a company, then you have to arrange pick-up times and payment plans.

As you begin to send out orders, you will find that many customers appreciate receiving e-mail verification of their order shipments and the ability to track their packages from your site on demand. Your follow-up e-mails might include information about the product, the final cost, date of shipment, estimated arrival date, tracking number, and contact information for customer service. All of this information can help a customer if there is a problem with the shipping.

Small businesses today can easily provide the delivery services that customers want and need. Special attention to handling and shipping orders makes for a satisfied customer, which often means a repeat buyer in the future.

OUTSOURCE, BUT NOT OUT OF CONTROL

Don't be afraid to outsource components of your Web site, such as the shopping cart, tracking customers, and handling transactions. Many pundits advise against this, but there's little downside risk. This is not so different from a bricks and mortar business contracting to have cleaning or payroll services.

Visitors who come to your site and decide to buy a product need to merely click "add to my purchase" or "add to shopping cart." This links them to your outsourcing service: a secure server who receives the visitor's credit card and contact information and completes the transaction for you. When the visitors are finished shopping, they return to your Web site. After all, you want them to keep browsing.

Outsourcing doesn't force you to relinquish control. Actually, you maintain complete control of your Web pages on the server that you have selected. You're able to maintain flexibility and are free from handling routine transactions. The site visitor is able to make purchases quickly and easily, and what appears to be seamless, may still linger on your site. It is a win-win-win marketing strategy.

TEACH WHAT THEY WISH TO MASTER—ONLINE TUTORIALS

What else can help enhance your relationship with site visitors? How about online tutorials? These are short, to-the-point instructions that teach visitors something that is of interest to them or will be otherwise appreciated.

Web-based online training firms routinely offer tutorials, but virtually any other Web vendor can offer them as well. If you're in hardware and plumbing supply, you could offer a brief tutorial on how to fix a kitchen sink. If you're a French teacher, offer a lesson on active versus inactive verbs. If you are a drama coach, offer a short tutorial on properly using the stage for dramatic effect.

If you don't have the in-house capabilities for devising such a tutorial, options are available right in your local area. Many college students,

Tutorials can come in many forms. They could be screens that lead visitors from one step to the next, punctuated by text or audio. They could follow a standard outline or have a "game-show" type of format, or be led by an online cartoon type figure. The options are almost endless.

particularly those who are majoring in graphics, communications, or computer science have the background and capability to devise short programs for you that are effective and affordable.

Such programs are usually shown on the opening Web page, with a message such as "click here for online tutorial," or "click here for demo." The visitor clicks and is whisked away down highly friendly paths, where they only have to make minimal input, while obtaining a glimpse as to how your system works, or how to perform a certain task, like repair the kitchen sink.

As with other Web site marketing techniques, offering an online tutorial positions you as an expert in the field. If you can tutor someone over the Web as to how to fix a kitchen sink, you certainly can fix a kitchen sink yourself. The implication is that you can fix a lot more as well. Some people who take your tutorial will decide that they don't necessarily want to fix the kitchen sink themselves, after all. So, they will call you. Likewise for any other instruction guides you post on your Web site.

START A GIFT REGISTRY AND REAP

Brick-and-mortar retailers have long known that gift registries are an excellent way to build name recognition, generate new customers, create goodwill, and boost sales. With the advent of the Internet, Web businesses have discovered that gift registries and Web marketing are a natural fit for each other. The name of the game is consumer convenience, and Web-based gift registries have the game down pat.

Many retailers who had gift registry programs before the Internet, such as J.C. Penney, Pier I Imports, and Crate and Barrel, have updated their gift registries to take advantage of the Web. For instance, Pier I's Web site at pier1.com contains updated information on all Pier I gift registries in the United States. After registrants open a registry in a Pier I store, they can use the Web site to make changes and additions to the registry. Shoppers can use the Web site to view the registry and make purchases from it.

Crate and Barrel's Web site, crateandbarrel.com, features similar functionality, as well as a promise that in the near future, new registrants will be able to register online, taking convenience to the next level.

You don't have to have a large department store to benefit from incorporating a gift registry into your Web site. Specialty food and drink retailers, soap and candle makers, booksellers, clothiers, music distributors—if you've got a wide enough range of products, you can operate a successful gift registry.

Even if you're not a typical consumer-goods retailer, a gift registry still could be useful to you. Service providers are especially well-suited for gift registries. For instance, a massage therapist who operates as a sole-proprietor and has their own Web site could offer a wide variety of spa services, such as massages, facials, pedicures, and aroma-therapy treatments as items on a gift registry.

When setting up a gift registry on the Web, functionality is crucial. Is the registry updated to reflect purchases? Does the site provide click-through buying? If the registry can't reliably deliver the kind of convenience shoppers are looking for, they'll take their business somewhere else. Be sure the site works as advertised before you roll it out. A well-functioning Web-based gift registry can enhance your status and strengthen your business, both on the Web and off.

EXTEND AND SUPPLEMENT YOUR IN-STORE SALES

Any size business can use the Internet to enrich sales. *Lands' End*, the oft-cited direct marketer of traditional, casual, and business clothing, uses a multitude of hyperlinked, interactive pages on its Web site to enhance the print catalog. "The Web site is a way we can reinforce what's in our catalog," says Ron Frey, Lands' End's Internet Business Manager. "It's an extension to our catalog."

Land's End's site is loaded with details and information that would be cost-prohibitive to carry in every catalog, not to mention the fact that it would require a weight lifter's muscles to pick up and read. Yet, even though the site generates lots of traffic and its electronic transactions are increasing, the company still depends heavily on catalog sales.

The Web site is dependent upon customers to come to it, whereas the catalog is sent to customers. Furthermore, people still like to flip through printed pages at a leisurely pace over a cup of morning coffee, and enjoy the instant give-and-take of speaking directly to a sales representative when placing an order.

You can also use cybersales to supplement your in-store sales. Located in Eugene, Oregon in a historic commercial building converted to upscale shops and restaurants, the Cotton Mill specializes in comfortable, quality cotton clothing. Ed Reiman, the store's proprietor, uses his

Web site as an electronic catalog. He used to give his customers, many of them from out-of-town, a print brochure with product and ordering information, but found it difficult to keep current. Now he hands out business cards directing people to his site.

No, people can't go to his online store, feel the fabric, try on the clothes for fit, and have personal advice from the owner. But once customers have visited the real store and sampled the merchandise firsthand, they can, and do, easily order more from the electronic catalog.

TOUT YOUR STORE-TO-DOOR DELIVERY SERVICES

With less time on their hands, people are more likely to use a service that offers free delivery, especially if it comes with a within-the-hour guarantee. Joseph Park, chairman and CEO of kozmo.com, knew this when he started his New York-based business.

> With the pace of life steadily increasing, a huge market for delivery services has emerged.

Park's business offers a variety of services, including video rentals, magazine purchases, CD purchases, and, their most popular feature, snack purchases. The items that Park and his colleagues make available are typical impulse items, like the ones found in the checkout line at the grocery store.

Almost all consumers are enticed by the occasional impulse buy. Kozmo.com simply makes this easier, putting cheap, fun items on the Web. These items attract customers, who find instant gratification without having to leave their homes or offices. With a few clicks, their impulse purchases can arrive for them within the hour.

Many companies are starting to offer similar delivery services. Whether they are grocery stores or book companies, most of these services boast a same-day or next-day guarantee, or they charge a fee for 30-minute or one-hour delivery. Park knew that few people would be interested in his service if they had to pay a delivery fee, especially when most of the products they sell are under $5.

Considering the impulse nature of the products offered by kozmo.com, Park also knew that few people would be interested in waiting a day or two for delivery. Thus the major draw of kozmo.com is the fast, free delivery.

Kozmo.com reveals some of the true potential of Web-based businesses to upset the apple-cart of old-school commerce. By providing fast-paced Internet purchasing and speedy local delivery, kozmo.com has expanded into an entirely new, unique market. This new company has tapped into an existent market in a new and unique way by using the Internet. Kozmo.com has expanded to Seattle, San Francisco, Boston, Los Angeles, and Washington, DC since its start, and plans to be available in 30 cities within the year. Meanwhile, Park also plans to continue expanding the product line.

While many fear that the Internet is ruining the traditional business world, companies such as kozmo.com show that the Internet is having more impact on business by opening up entirely new markets. Using the Internet, small business entrepreneurs have the ability to revolutionize almost any market in traditional business.

DONATE SPACE ALL OVER THE PLACE

When you allow users to create their own Web pages, it builds a sense of community for your business's Web page, in the same way that chat rooms and forums do. People naturally want to share the Web pages that they create with their family members, friends, and co-workers. If every member's Web site contains a link back to your company's home page, then you can count on gaining more traffic to your Web site. GeoCities at geocities.com was acquired by Yahoo! and represents one of the Web's largest communities.

Users have created more than 32 million Web pages through GeoCities, because the publishing tools are designed for nontechnical users. It is easy for them to create, publish, and update their pages.

A related idea for your Web site is offering a "create-a-Web-page" service to boost your online community. The idea here is to generate business. For example, if your company makes plumbing supplies and fixtures, you could allow plumbers to create their own business Web pages on your site. This would stimulate business because when the plumbers' customers go to their Web pages, they will be able to learn about your products and are more likely to want their plumbers to use them. It would be a great way to give your products a name among the people who are purchasing them.

Soon nearly any company will be able to act as an Internet service provider and therefore create an intimate and ongoing relationship with customers by providing the opportunity for customers and companies to

Allowing customers to create their own Web pages for free is a simple and manageable tactic now and will extend the reach of your advertising. Offering space to businesses that relate, but don't compete with yours, can also bring new traffic to your home page.

have strong and consistent interaction. K-mart has already discovered this community-building service with its free Internet service called BlueLight.com.

EVENT LISTING—USEFUL AND TIMELY

Consider the highly attractive feature of event listings, particularly if your Web site caters to a local area. With this technique, you make it known among your site visitors that you will post events of interest to them in a timely and prominent matter. These events will even include submissions from your visitors.

As with other features on your site, you may want to have a highly visible hyperlink on your opening page or simply start the event listing someplace in the opening page itself. Give site visitors a running lead, perhaps only posting events with four- to seven-day lead times.

As the number of events that you post grows, and the popularity in this feature becomes more widely known, you may find yourself attracting a loyal cadre of visitors who check in regularly for this particular feature. Each event could be hyperlinked so that visitors can attain detailed information.

Never mind that some of the links will throw them off of your page and onto someone else's. The service that you're providing ensures that

To draw attention to this feature, it may pay for you to include a small graphic with each listing. If there is a fair or expo, use a symbolic graphic of a merry-go-round or a Ferris-wheel. For something related to health, you can have a stethoscope, hypodermic needle, or eye chart.

they will come back over and over again, because, after all, you are the one doing the overall posting.

Offer a standing invitation including detailed information about how visitors post their events. You could briefly mention the opportunity for others to post their events at the top of your feature and refer to detailed information at the bottom of the feature, or simply hyperlink it. You can also automate the ability of visitors to post their events, although you will probably want to review and approve their enclosed lists of events, screen for appropriate language, and correct any grammatical errors.

A word to the unwary: Follow up on the accuracy of any events that you or others post. There is nothing worse than listing the wrong phone number or address, or having the wrong date or time to a posted event, and ending up causing site visitors to act upon wrong information. Such a transgression would be contrary to effective marketing, and likely to infuriate some.

When the accuracy and integrity of your event listing is demonstrated over and over again, you may find that you have a loyal following of regular visitors.

7

KEEPING CUSTOMERS HAPPY

I n any business, communication among employees and workers is important to the success of the company, but perhaps even more so in the newer, faster-moving e-business environment. Independent of the size of your company, communication skills among employees are essential to survival and success in the marketplace.

COMMUNICATION REMAINS THE KEY

Ed Harley, of Pandesic LLC, a joint venture between Intel and Sap that makes Web-hosting technology, admits that communication is a concern within companies such as his own. Harley revealed that with the constant impending product release deadlines and never-ending flow of ideas in the workplace, many employees fail to communicate their needs to one another.

Developing products and services requires cooperation. Harley found that informal group meetings between staff members helped deal with the communication issues at Pandesic. By giving employees the opportunity to focus on talking with each other, they were able to learn how they could help one another.

Similarly, Frederic Holzberger, CEO of Aveda/Fredric's found that holding weekly company-wide meetings improves productivity. Every Thursday, the entire 80-person staff meets in the education center, where they brainstorm and talk informally. Before the staff meeting, each department holds a smaller, more intimate meeting to discuss its own state of affairs. Holzberger finds that these staff meetings help employees develop better ways to serve customers.

WE'RE ALL INTERNET MANAGERS

In his book, *The Ten Second Internet Manager*, Mark Breier argues that every manager today is an Internet manager whether you are an Internet pioneer, a manufacturer, a retailer, or a service provider.

> The keys to being effective on the Internet are creating brand loyalty, truly caring about your customers, and making a continuing, steadfast effort to serve needs. If these sound like traditional strategies or clichés, they are. On the Web, however, effective Internet managers do them at warp speed by using e-mail and customer feedback.

The old cliché, "The customer is always right," is taken to a new level on the Web as well, with the customer being the sole determiner of the success or failure of a business. Often, this success or failure comes in a short time. Thus, it is important for a Web site to be as customer-friendly and helpful as possible. This can be done in several ways, the simplest of which is listening to the people who visit your site. This sounds absurd. How can one listen on a Web site? The answer is: ask. Most importantly, make it easy for your customers to answer.

LISTEN TO YOUR CUSTOMERS BY ASKING

Arriving at the initial page of Fool.com (a Web site devoted to helping customers track their investments and converse with other investors of all levels), the customer is immediately faced with several important things. First, a description of what the site offers. Second, an offer to become a member of the site (free of charge), allowing access to all that the site offers. Third, and most important, a short survey used to determine what type of investor the customer is and allow the customer access to the entire site.

Upon filling out the initial survey, the customer is asked to fill out another, more detailed survey that is used to determine what the customer wants from the site and how the site can assist the customer in fulfilling their needs. In other words, Fool.com is determining its target customer base, learning information on its site visitors, and deciding how it can better fit the needs of the consumer.

With this information, Fool.com can offer individual services through its partner site, Datek Online, specific to a consumer's needs. With simple survey tools, Fool.com has discovered who its consumer is, what the consumer wants and needs, and how it can increase the site's utility.

Your survey should be simple and easy to answer. On Fool.com, answers are provided. Customers merely have to click on the answers that apply to them. The questions you pose should allow you to quickly determine who your customers are and what they want or need from your site.

Make the survey worth the customer's time. One way to do this is by making your customer feel like an individual, not just a target audience. Offering them individual assistance or a personal response via e-mail, telephone, or snail mail is an option.

To be competitive in the Internet market, a business has to determine who its consumers are, listen to their wants and needs, and individually provide for them. In doing so, a business gives the consumer a positive picture of the company, and encourages them to return to the site and utilize its applications.

A STAPLE IN MARKETING: PROVIDE SERVICE AND CONVENIENCE

With more technology, Internet consumers come to the marketplace with increasing expectations of companies' abilities to serve them. Consumers want everything, from products to services, to be quicker and better. This shift in consumer attitude is prompting some companies to revolutionize the systems used by the most established business and service providers.

Andrew Krainin's company, Shipper.com, is changing the face of the delivery and shipping world. Krainin realized that with the speed and convenience of Internet shopping, customers are becoming impatient with the slow and costly service of the shipping industry. His new company makes same-day shipping an affordable service. Rates begin at about $5 for areas served by Shipper.com.

To provide this service, Shipper.com uses a revolutionary system. The company stores fast-moving products like books, music, and electronics, in distribution centers in larger cities that it serves. Shipper.com also uses its own fleet of delivery vehicles, which sometimes completes orders that come with special shipping instructions.

The company doesn't necessarily challenge the traditional shipping companies, but rather, offers complimentary services that accommodate the needs of an existing market. In changing the traditional system, Shipper.com challenges traditional shipping companies by targeting a market heretofore ignored.

NowDocs.com has challenged the local print shop in a similar manner, offering a new breed of copying and courier services to the business world. Going to the Web site, customers can choose the destination of a document, choose a delivery timetable, and load their work to be formatted and printed. After viewing the document in "print preview," the customer can choose among various binding and printing options. With this service, customers can save valuable working time by avoiding tedious trips to the print shop and courier office.

> All Web-based businesses face the challenge to serve their customers in unique and satisfying ways. For small business entrepreneurs this means recognizing the most unique way that you can serve the market. Not every new business has to offer a new product or service, but most can offer new methods for handling old situations.

MAKE ONLINE SHOPPING EASY AND SAFE

If your business offers some type of product that can be bought online, there are several ways to make the purchasing process an easy and positive experience for your customers. Like all consumers, Internet buyers talk to each other. More than anything else, people tend to share their negative buying experiences, and these stories influence their friends. As a Web-based merchant, aim for excellent service, so that no one can say anything negative about it. Shopping on your site needs to be easy, safe, and honest.

Building trust with your customers is the only way that they will return to shop again and tell others about the ease, convenience, and dependability of shopping on your site. Trust is built through security. Any transaction on your site needs to be over a secure server. Initially, this allows the customer to feel safe about entering personal information such as addresses and credit card numbers.

When browsing your site, customers should not have to search for prices and shipping charges. Let them know all of this information up front and with every item offered. If you don't, you make the shopping experience difficult and possibly frustrating for the customer. If you believe in the products and services you offer, you have nothing to hide from your customers.

Offer a way that customers can register with your site, so that they do not have to reenter all of their personal information for every purchase they make. This is a rather simple addition. Customers register with your site, entering all of their personal information (name, address, etc.), and receive a user-name and password. When this user-name and password are reentered for a later purchase, their stored information is attached to the new purchase and you have made their experience that much easier.

Ensure that customers are given and understand your return/exchange policy before the time of purchase. Make returns and exchanges as easy as possible.

The key to building a solid customer base that shops regularly on your site with trust and confidence in your company is to make the experience as easy and safe as possible. If you only give a customer positive things to say, then your business can only experience positive results.

Consider hereafter that anytime a Web visitor makes the leap and decides to do business with your company, you have the wonderful opportunity to initiate a relationship that could turn into a long-term customer. An Internet-driven prospect essentially wants the same as any prospect: Most people want to know that they're dealing with a company of integrity. That means totally accurate product and service descriptions, on-time delivery, and a reasonable return policy.

REFUNDS NEEDN'T BE PAINFUL

Returns and refunds are a customer-friendly aspect of your Web site. You read it correctly. If you offer any product, then undoubtedly you'll be presenting comprehensive ordering information, a privacy policy, and some type of guarantee. When people order items over the Web, they haven't had a chance to physically inspect them, so you have to allow for a higher percentage of returns than would otherwise occur in a bricks and mortar retail store.

By prominently posting your returns and refunds policy, you help to put customers at ease. You tell them that you have a highly professional business, and you place the customer's needs at the forefront of your product and service offerings. You understand that occasionally even the most honest, conscientious customers can make an ordering mistake, and the product or service that they receive may not match their expectations.

The experience of most vendors offering such return policies is that only a small fraction of customers ever take them up on it. Still, it is a highly effective marketing vehicle to have such a policy in place for customer reassurance, even if for no other reason.

Here is some sample wording that you could employ in designing your own return/refund policy:

What about our return policy?

You may return any item in its original condition within 15 days of receiving it for a full refund. We only refund shipping costs if the return is a result of our error. Please wrap the package securely and return it using Insured Parcel Post or UPS ground tracking service (800-xxx-xxxx).

Even the smoothest online ordering system has its difficulties compared with a shopper's ability to handle a product in a store. People may need to frequently return or exchange products. Why not reduce the customer's risk to ZERO? Given your ability to collect payment via credit card, cybercash type systems, or customer check all prior to your having to submit the goods and services, it is the customer, and not you, who is at risk. Therefore, it behooves you to lower the customer's risk as much as possible.

Zero customer risk is most desirable. If you doubt this, think of the times when you are the customer ordering goods from long distance. Do you want to be taken? How does it feel when you are deceived? Is it frustrating to receive the wrong item, or an item of far lesser quality than you were led to believe? If these situations are frustrating for you, how

I f you make any mistake with a purchase or return, be honest about it, apologize for it, and offer some retribution for the hassle you have caused.

can you not do everything in your power to reduce a customer's risk in doing business with you?

KEEP YOUR ORDERING SYSTEM SIMPLE

In the days of yore, when businesses relied on printed catalogs, brochures, pamphlets, flyers, and fax items, there was a limit to how much you could include in terms of product and service offerings. On your Web site, for all intents and purposes, you have an infinite number of pages with which to supply customers with product and service information.

Having the ability to offer elaborate, extensive descriptions of a multitude of products and services does not necessarily mean that you should. Consider your own experience as a consumer, particularly visiting a Web site that offered too much on every page. It's easy to be overwhelmed if there are too many hyperlinks to click or too many products or services coming in too many variations to consider.

The natural response to information overload is to shut down, to have an inability to choose. Some customers will leave the Web site, because they find overly complex product/service options to be not worth the time and effort. Others may stick with the complexity, while being somewhat resentful that it takes so much time to find what they want.

You want to give your customers choices, but not so many that the typical customer ends up feeling abused by too many, rather than being served by a manageable number. In my book, *The Complete Idiot's Guide to Managing Stress*, I explain at length how too many choices has become a significant problem for most people. So offer a variety of choices, but take great pains not to offer so many that you lose customers. How many choices? It depends on what you are offering, but for a quick estimate survey friends, relatives, and frequent customers as to what they deem appropriate.

If you sell camping supplies, for example, perhaps 8 to 16 types of pup tents will do as opposed to 24 or 48. The same could be said of lanterns, sleeping bags, and other supplies. Then you can always arrange your pages so that customers who actually enjoy dealing with hundreds of options with nitty-gritty detail can click on and on to satisfy their information quests. For your customers' ease, however, keep it simple, focus on your most popular items, and have the mental and emotional strength not to inundate visitors simply because you can.

While on the topic of keeping it simple for visitors, make sure that every page on your site will take them back to your home page, the previous page, or some other value-packed page. In other words, give visitors simple options to make them feel and indeed put them in control.

If a visitor becomes lost or sidetracked while visiting your site, you don't want to take the chance that they will move on to somebody else's because they are too frustrated mastering the rigors of navigating your site. So visit each and every page of your site. Walk through it slowly and carefully to ensure that any visitor will quickly return to something familiar and comfortable or can move forward to something that appears to bring great value.

OFFER BENEFITS FOR LOYAL CUSTOMERS

Loyalty deserves to be rewarded. Loyalty benefits have proven effective for many companies and businesses in the past. A customer loyalty program, put simply, is any program that offers benefits or rewards to customers who regularly use a product or service from a particular company.

The most widely recognized examples of customer loyalty programs are the frequent flyer awards offered by many airlines. With airlines, the frequent flyer miles can be free trips or flight miles toward trips, special memberships, preferred seating, gifts, and so on. More and more companies are realizing that they can create programs with the same basic idea: reward customers and they will keep coming back.

> Loyalty programs work because they reward continuous customers and show them your appreciation. They also motivate new customers, perhaps not yet qualified, to strive to receive the benefits.

The special benefits can vary as much as they do with the airlines. For example, you can offer discounts for customers who spend above a certain level of money on your products or services. This will bring in more money for you, and allow the customer to feel better about spending more money.

There are certain principles of loyalty marketing, all of which apply if you intend to set up a program on your Web page. First, use incentives and awards to keep a customer for life. This way you increase the percent of each customer's total purchases of products or services in your category. Most of all, realize that it costs you less to retain a customer than it does to acquire a new one. Once you understand these principles, you can start to see the difference that a customer loyalty program can make for your business.

Another way to reward your valued customers is to set up a members-only domain on your Web site. Here, you can win the loyalty of a select group of people by giving them special access to premium services. You can make the members-only domain password-protected.

Membership can be based on the amount of previous purchases, or any other qualification that you see fit.

> Once a preferred customer becomes a member, continue to give them access to discounts or other special offers. They will be more likely to remain a customer if they feel that you appreciate their business and reward them fairly for their loyalty.

Whatever method you choose, your company or business can greatly benefit from offering rewards to loyal customers. As customers purchase your products and services, they become increasingly pleased with the quality they enjoy and the appreciation and rewards that you give them. Both loyalty programs and members-only benefits increase the probability that a customer will keep doing business with you.

MAKE SHOPPING ON YOUR SITE A PLEASURE

Walter Arnold is an artist and a businessman. Carving in stone since age 12, he honed his artistry by apprenticing with master carvers in Italy. He went on to work on the National Cathedral in Washington, DC. Now, Arnold has a thriving studio in the Chicago area, and a successful storefront on the Web. One of the first to recognize the potential of the Internet, he set up shop in cyberspace in August 1994—a site loaded with information and graphics about himself, his craft, and his stunning work.

Today, Arnold's site, www.stonecarver.com, includes a shopping cart. A look at how Arnold manages his e-commercial activity shows how e-commerce can be a viable and profitable endeavor for any business—from retailing to stone carving.

In addition to filling commissions for original custom sculptures (fireplaces, architectural ornaments, signs, and public and personal pieces, to name a few), Arnold sells quality reproductions of a selection of his gargoyles, ranging in price from $5 to $345. To accommodate online patrons, he set up an electronic shopping cart using CartCart, a $140 software package.

Though the software's standard setup, using ready-made templates, is fairly quick and easy, Arnold spent four days recoding and customizing the pages, scripts, and forms. "I wanted to tune into the interface throughout the site, making the process as smooth and simple as possible, so people wouldn't hit delays and move on," Arnold said. "I didn't want the site to get in the way of the sale."

> To make sure it worked as smoothly as he intended, he had testers run through the ordering process while he observed. Any flaws he noticed were fixed immediately.

"Try to look at the whole ordering process through the customer's eyes," cautions Arnold, "not your eyes. After setup, listen carefully to what your customers say," and revise the design and procedures accordingly.

Each online order comes into Arnold by e-mail, containing everything except the customer's credit card number. Instead, the number is encrypted and sent to a designated spot on Arnold's service provider's server, which he then accesses through a secure connection. "If people aren't comfortable with giving their credit card number online, they can submit a dummy number and I'll call them later for the real one," notes Arnold.

He then manually processes each credit card offline, and, after verifying the card's authenticity and credit availability, confirms receipt of the order by e-mail. Once the item is shipped, he sends another e-mail with the shipment's tracking number.

Though efficient enough for low-volume sales, e-tailers expecting substantial online activity would do well to automate order acceptance and confirmation. Your software needs to contain interactive scripts to handle immediate online confirmation, and a gateway can manage credit card processing directly from your Web site. Three companies offering such gateway services are CyberSource, Authorize.net, and Signio.

Even here, where a lot of personalization is required, Arnold uses the Internet extensively to develop and complete the piece according to his customers' wishes. Some 90 percent of customer communication is done by e-mail. Arnold even e-mails pictures of the design and photos of progressive stages of a fireplace for customer input. For people who might have difficulty dealing with a graphics file attached to an e-mail, he sets up a special page on his site and tells them where to find it.

You can also gain more users by personalizing your site. Choose the graphics and style that you think are appropriate for the type of people you are seeking to attract. By personalizing your site in this way, customers will be more interested in what you have to offer.

8

KEEPING THE TRAIN RUNNING

All too often, entrepreneurs become caught up in the excitement and novelty of launching their sites, which is understandable. In the first weeks and months after a site goes up much attention is given to all aspects of it.

As the months roll by, a curious but predictable phenomenon ensues. In all too many businesses the Web site is treated with benign neglect. After all, we did a great job; we arranged a highly effective, user-friendly site that meets the needs of our targeted niche. What more do we have to do? As it turns out, you have to inspect your site on a regular basis, because, quite frankly, things change.

> It seems obvious, but it's vital to keep your site updated. Updating it at least monthly is good, although weekly is preferable, and more often than that is highly desirable.

UPDATE DESPITE THE TIME CRUNCH

Your market changes; people's needs change; technology changes; society changes. All of this ensures that something on your site will appear dated or stale. The moment this happens, the overall marketing value of your site begins to decline. Not every visitor may notice or care. Some do. We've all seen wonderful sites that carried some trend or news update section with a date that was three months old.

When parties to whom you are referring, such as elected officials, are no longer in office, the year changes, or anything else in society changes, you have to be aware of this and consider the impact that it could have on your Web site. At least annually, it makes sense to go through every single page, and change all copyright notices to the current year.

It also makes sense to revisit all links to make sure that they are active. In any given year, at least 20 percent of the links that you may have posted no longer lead to the Web site you intended to offer your visitors. This is because other sites change their addresses or go out of business.

If you list any price information, review it all again to ensure that you are posting accurate information. If you have voluminous text on your site, and feel that proofreading everything once again for accuracy and currency is too big a task for you, then print all of the pages of your site and hire a part-time editor who will carefully review all of your text.

Even if nothing has changed in society or in the marketplace, and the dates or prices or other numbers you have listed are all valid, it still pays to have an editor review the printout pages of your site to ensure that you are offering syntactically and grammatically correct verbage.

Keeping your site up-to-date and accurate may not seem like a glamorous task, or even like a front-burner marketing issue, yet it is one that you cannot afford to ignore. Visitors take it as a given that dynamic, effective businesses have sites that are equally dynamic and effective. If yours is a wee bit stale, it opens up the doors for visitors to go someplace else.

NOT THE BE-ALL AND END-ALL

Is your site the be-all and end-all point of marketing? For many entrepreneurs, the answer is no. "The Web site is the introduction to what will hopefully be a beautiful, long-lasting relationship," says Dan Janal, at janal.com, an internationally respected Internet marketer and author who delivers keynotes and training seminars.

The reason, Janal observes, "is that you can't expect people to come back to your Web site on a regular basis. They are simply too busy. Sure, people will come back to their stock broker's site to check their finances, or the news site to see what's up, or the sports sites to follow their teams, but there is little reason for a consumer to return to a general commerce site. In fact, with all the competition on the Web, you're lucky to attract them to your site even once!"

What's a business to do? Janal suggests that entrepreneurs use e-mail in their marketing programs. The best marketing strategy on the Web is to create a newsletter or magazine and send it by e-mail. The newsletter can contain articles that help the readers do their jobs better, as well as offer them discounts on your products and services. The benefit for you is that you'll be able to keep in touch with your customers and prospects on a regular basis for a low cost.

"E-mail marketing programs have been shown to be extremely effective," says Janal. "With a homegrown list, research shows that 65 percent of the people will open the e-mail and 35 percent of them will take some form of action suggested in the message, such as link to a Web page, see a product demo online, or buy the product. You can't beat those numbers!"

While people won't revisit a Web site often, they certainly do open their e-mail boxes every day to see what's there.

Creating your own mailing list is easy. Janal suggests that you post a notice on your Web site stating that your customers can join your mailing list for free simply by providing their e-mail addresses. Promote your mailing list in your print publications and personal contacts as well.

> You don't want to ask too many questions as people zealously guard their privacy.

Next, Janal advises, tell them what benefits they will derive from reading your newsletter: offers on special products, news about their industries, and help-tips to more effectively use your products are good topics. "Also, let them know that you won't sell the names on the list to other companies. People hate when you do that. In fact, the number one reason people don't join lists is because they are afraid of getting more junk e-mail."

Now, you have to write the newsletter. Keep your articles short; your readers can't or don't want to handle too much. "Around 500 words or less should do it. Use bullets and lists to make the article more readable for a screen format," says Janal.

Finally, Janal recommends that you ask people to forward the newsletter to their colleagues who would be interested in this subject matter. You'll find that pass-along power of the Net to be among the most valuable tools.

If you follow Janal's advice, you'll build a loyal following of readers who will be happy to recommend their colleagues to your business. You can contact Dan Janal directly at dan@janal.com.

SYNDICATE YOUR ARTICLES THE EASY WAY

What if there were an easy way to have your articles regularly read on thousands of Internet sites? Tom Antion, who is considered one of the top small business Internet marketers, says, "In the recent past you would have little chance to make that happen easily."

Antion contends that you would have to contact the sites to make the deal and then e-mail them an article each week or at any interval upon which you decide. Then, you would have to hope that each site makes the updates in a timely fashion...ha!

"Fat chance of that happening," he says. "Making the deal in the first place would be hard enough because most people that have Web sites depend upon Webmasters to make changes again. Try getting the average Webmaster to respond quickly and regularly. Even if the site owner updated their own site, you are talking about lots of work doing regular updates, until now."

Enter an inexpensive piece of software called Master Syndicator, at mastersyndicator.com. You can have this software installed for about $150. Antion advises, "You write your articles and put them in the supplied Web page. Instantly, all the sites that have accepted your articles are updated. The sites that use your articles have zero work other than to put one line of code in their Web site one time. After that, there is no maintenance."

Consider the power this brings to your desktop at home. "Each deal you make with another Web site means that all its visitors are being exposed to your ideas, products, and services on a regular basis, which means money in your bank account," says Antion. "Lots of money if you play your cards right. You are also providing fresh content for the sites hosting your articles. Everyone wins."

Antion can be reached at tom@antion.com or antion.com and he offers hundreds of such ideas at his Butt Camp, antion.com/buttcamp.htm.

AUTO REMOVAL: NOT ABOUT REMOVING JUNK CARS

A pleasant development on the Web, specifically related to magazines, is enabling recipients to unsubscribe to what you send them. The auto removal feature that wise 'zine publishers offer to their recipients is more than a mere convenience. It conveys a message to recipients that you value and respect their time and attention, and their right to control their own inboxes.

> By including the auto removal feature with each issue of the 'zine that you send out, you can convey to your recipients that you are a service-oriented company, even if it means making it easy for others to get you out of their lives.

INSTANT ALERTS

Whether or not you disseminate a periodic 'zine, sometimes you get wind of information that is so important to your clients or customers that you simply have to alert them. Devise a special e-mail format, perhaps labeled "Instant Alert," so that your customers grasp the importance of the message that you're sending.

Don't overuse this promotional vehicle. If you publish a biweekly magazine (sending information 26 times a year to the targeted recipients), then three or four times a year during the off week, offer an instant alert. Sending alerts more often than that runs the risk of having your alerts not seem like alerts at all.

What you choose to send needs to be unique based on the characteristics and needs of your recipients. Here, however, are some general guidelines:

- Check out the information thoroughly, on your own end, before sending it.
- Keep your alert short and highly targeted. A paragraph is good; a short paragraph is even better. Include any contact information including toll-free numbers, or Web sites in your alert so recipients can follow up immediately.
- Devote one phrase or sentence to the importance of the message. For example: "This is important because XYZ."
- Indicate if there are any time related opportunities, like "This offer expires in three days."
- Include only a modest trailer to the alert, offering your name and contact information.

If one of your alerts happens to coincide with the dissemination of your periodic 'zine then, of course, put it at the top of the 'zine and then follow with the regular format.

MAKE YOUR SITE "STICKIER"

Earlier in the life of Internet marketing it was held that the greatest task that every Web site builder faces is making a site "sticky." At the zenith of the dotcom hype, pundits claimed that making your site sticky is the end-all of effective Web marketing. The prevailing thought was that the longer a visitor stays, the more valuable your site has to be. If visitors stay long enough, well by golly, your Web site is probably truly engaging.

The problem with such thinking is that how long visitors happen to linger on your site doesn't necessarily equate with the effectiveness of your site particularly in terms of your marketing goals. Ask your book-keeper or accountant how many sales and what volume was generated as a result of your site visitors.

The truth lies somewhere in the middle. Sticky sites have the ability to keep the attention of visitors. If a visitor clicks onto your site and then immediately clicks off to another site, you have accomplished nothing. You need to find ways to keep your visitors interested long enough to accomplish your goal—presumably to do business with you in some capacity.

Avoid luring your customers with gimmicks and sales pitches; feed them with the quality information that many other sites fail to offer.

Many tools can help keep your site sticky, but these are only worthwhile if they keep meeting your customers' needs. You may have a chat room where visitors can talk with other Internet users, with any luck, about how wonderful your product is. Other tools may include interactive polls, Web-based calendars that visitors can set up and use, auctions, etc.

Take eBay.com as an example. According to NetRatings, a traffic analysis firm, eBay's average visitor spends one hour and five minutes on its site. The reason for this is that the site offers easy navigational tools, gives visitors information on how to use the site, and makes the visitor's overall experience an easy and positive one.

What is the best way to make your site sticky? Provide your visitors with good information about your product. This might include studies that have been done on your product, testaments from other customers who have purchased your product, or general, rich information about your product and not another sales pitch.

> While it's vital to give your visitors a reason to buy your product, it will be more beneficial to you if that reason is given by way of factually based information and previous customer approval.

Ultimately, if you are not meeting net income goals then all is for naught. There are a variety of reasons that a visitor might stay at your site for an extended period of time, but that doesn't necessarily add up to revenues. Keep focusing on fundamentals, such as offering convenience, ease of access, and great values.

HIGHLIGHT YOUR URL EVERY DAY IN EVERY WAY

Do you interact in person with potential clients and customers? For example, brokers often hold public seminars or forums, free of charge, to invited members of the general public who want to increase their net worth. Increasingly, doctors, especially eye doctors offering Lasik surgery, dentists, and others in the medical professions are doing the same. Insurance agents, computer consultants, and other professionals who offer highly specialized services do so as well.

When presenting to any such group, and using any type of participant packets, handout materials, overheads, or slides, make sure that your URL is listed on every artifact.

- Put the Web site address on all visuals such as overheads, slides, LCD projected visuals, photos, charts, graphs, and exhibits.
- Put your Web address on any information booklets, packets, pamphlets, flyers, or handouts.
- Be sure to have the address on each and every page since participants will sometimes disassemble a package and maintain only those pages relative to them.
- Put your Web site on any other type of handout, bonus giveaway, gift, or premium, as well.
- During your presentation refer to your Web site a couple of times and have a visual ready that actually shows one or more pages.
- Whenever you announce such forums, be sure to include your Web site address in the announcement, press release, bulletin, newsletter, or other mode of information dissemination.

The principle behind this focused recommendation is that people have to know of your Web site to visit it. With millions of sites to choose from, a single exposure or single mention of your site is not likely to be sufficient to induce people to visit. They need to be exposed to the site several times. Combined with the promise of achieving a more favorable future for having visited your site, they gain critical information, save money, save time, or gain some other substantial benefit.

RECIPROCAL LINKS AND 40 WINKS

Joining up with another Web site so that you tout their site and they tout yours is a match made in cyberheaven. The cost of linking with

> Depending on what products and services you offer, there may be a variety of other suppliers, complementary product or service vendors, and supporting resources about which your customers would be privileged to know.

reciprocal sites is virtually nothing, and more people will be steered to your site, even while you sleep.

By having a special section on your site that links to all of these recommended Web sites, you do your customers a big favor. At the same time, you forge alliances with each of the parties you chose to recommend on your site. The ideal situation occurs when each of your participants gives equal time, space, and promotion to one another. Then, visitors who land on such reciprocating links and sites are far more inclined to make a visit to yours.

Through various tracking services such as Webtracker.com and Webgarage.com you can quickly determine the origin of your visitors. If it turns out that a handful of key sites count for many visitors, then strive to strengthen these relationships even further. Perhaps you can persuade the reciprocating party to include an extended paragraph about you, and offer the same in return.

Periodically visit these sites to which you are reciprocally linked. Make sure you are mentioned and positioned on their sites in an appropriate manner. Also, keep your reciprocal links informed as to major changes occurring in your company in terms of product and service offerings, Web design, and other benefits and features. This may not make a difference among those who may include a link to your site but it still makes sense to keep your reciprocal links informed. Besides, after devising the template e-mail with the update, it costs no more to send to one link or dozens.

Consider calling your linked recommended suppliers or members of your "partners program." This conveys to your visitors that you have an active and ongoing relationship with the parties to whom you are linked and can recommend them with confidence.

If you have the time and inclination, make an onsite visit to your partner's premises. To get your partner's program in high gear, exchange "tifs" or "jpegs" in addition to the link; also post a photo.

VIEWS ON NEWS GROUPS

What if you could venture out into the Internet and "recruit" visitors to your site as a result of messages you post? News groups, officially known as Usenet news groups, distribute messages called articles on specific subjects using the Internet. They are popular sources of information containing an estimated one million new articles posted each day. Your online marketing plan can benefit from the combination of global reach and interest that news groups offer.

Dejanews at dejanews.com, offers a quick and easy way to get up to speed regarding what any particular news group has been discussing. You also can type in key words and instantly be shown all the news groups with any ongoing discussion on the topic.

News groups are grouped by subject. When you post an article, you post it to the news groups of your choice, and it becomes viewable by all users. You can also send a reply to the author of a message to address a question, concern, or complaint. You can read articles in news groups without posting anything.

To use news groups to the advantage of your business or company, you may want to conduct some research on them. One research idea is looking around to find out if your competition uses news groups because it is a type of competitive intelligence to know what your competitors are doing. You can use research to find the ones in which you would like to participate. You also can find out if people are talking about your company or business.

To conduct research, you can use two types of searches. Search for news groups with names that relate to your product or service. Also search for any articles in all forums that mention the name of your product or service, specifically mentioning your company or your competition.

When you find groups that seem to encompass your target market, make an effort to monitor them regularly. You need to be familiar with the group before you become "conversant."

If you decide to post messages, you want to make sure that they succeed in communicating effectively. To do this, make the subject clear and keep it under 40 characters. Avoid misleading subjects; focus on the real issue. This is also true for the text of the message. Two to four paragraphs is sufficient to say what you need to say and is all the average online reader will be likely to read—do not be blatantly commercial. Include links to your Web page as appropriate so that all an interested reader has to do to access more information is click.

With these ideas in mind, news groups can allow you to track the trends in your field of online business and also gain more access to potential customers.

POST CARD CAMPAIGNS WORK WONDERS

Using post cards is a time-honored marketing technique for getting people interested in what you have to offer, or in this case, simply steering them to your Web site.

Why bother to mail target recipients information about your Web site via a post card at all? Because on a typical day, and even during a typical week, your intended recipients receive few, if any, post cards touting an individual Web site. The 4-inch by 6-inch size is recommended over the 3-inch by 5-inch, since the larger card has much more impact at the same mailing rate.

With post cards, you have the option of making a highly unique invitation. You could handwrite on each card, even if they are preprinted, thereby personalizing the card for each recipient. You can also include stars, buttons, banners, and any item that will both personalize and make your card stand out in the recipients' mail that day.

To make your mailing even more effective:

- Use a headline on both sides of the post card.
- Use initial caps only. All caps are too hard to read.
- Leave some white space. Even a post card can be too cluttered.

Also, experiment with changing the title of the card to appeal to targeted groups such as accountants, bankers, farmers, and whoever else you're seeking to reach.

> The key to using press releases effectively is to develop a story that allows you to talk about your site.

ANNOUNCE YOUR NEWS VIA PRESS RELEASES

Both your Web site and your company can gain exposure with press releases. Customers, investors, and members of the general public will have a chance to hear about your business if your press release is picked up by local media, national media, or both.

In your press release, describe the activities of your Web site. You can cite the number of daily visitors you receive, and you can describe new e-commerce features. Your press release can be made available over the Internet using traditional press release mediums like Business Wire at businesswire.com and PR Newswire at prnewswire.com. Press releases that appear on the Internet can include links to your Web pages for quick access and photographs that illustrate your business or services.

An effective press release might also be picked up by sites like Nasdaq at nasdaq.com and Microsoft Investor at investor.msn.com, where a variety of people can read about your product or service. There also are industry-focused organizations and e-'zines that request news. You can use a press release service that distributes your release to all of these sites.

Sending your release directly to newspapers, magazines, radio stations, and television stations through media contacts is another way to send your message to the public. Although this used to be a terribly difficult and time-consuming task, Paul Krupin has created the *U.S. All Media E-Mail Directory* to assist you. It is a publication with almost 12,000 e-mail addresses of contacts in magazines, newspapers, syndicates, radio, and television in the United States and Canada. They are organized by medium, contact name, and title. Using this service, you can pinpoint the contacts that might be interested in your press release.

Y ou want to avoid sending the press release to individuals who will find it worthless. By selecting likely media organizations, you avoid the offense and wasted time.

You can learn about the directory and find links to the Web pages of more than 3,000 magazines at owt.com/dircon.

If you focus your efforts and do some research, a press release can make people notice you. In the right place, a press release can catch the eye of a prospective customer, an investor, or another individual with something to offer to your organization.

ASSEMBLE YOUR LINEUP OF TEST VISITORS

Develop allies who can give you critical input to ensure that you have a highly marketable site. Specifically, you want allies to give you the critical input you need to make your site more appealing and useful to your visitors.

It is hard to be the sole judge of your own Web site's effectiveness. The more input you receive from your target market, the greater your objectivity will be. Consider asking:

- *Web specialists.* They can tell you things you wouldn't have heard elsewhere. Although many are techno-twits with no flair for design, some have the whole package knowledge of html, java, and Perl, and a tremendous sense of how to build an attractive, eye-catching site that people will want to revisit.

- *Previous and current clients* as well as anyone in the industry who will be responsive. These are key sources of feedback. Treat them well.

- *Peers.* Other home-business marketers can help you enormously. In particular, ask those who do not compete with you.

What do you ask your test visitors? Here are some ideas:

- Did the site load quickly enough for you?
- Was it visually appealing?
- Were you able to navigate it easily?
- Are the photos and icons appropriate?
- What feature did you like best?
- What feature did you like least?
- How does it compare with other sites?
- What would you like to see?
- What would make you return?
- What else can you suggest?

Be sure to reward your test visitors, particularly right after they have given you their feedback. You want to do this for several reasons, first being that it makes good sense to give value for value. Beyond that, however, as you make changes and updates to your Web site, you want to be able to go back to some of these same people, particularly the experts among your test visitors, and ask them to do another walk-through.

If you reinforce their behavior by giving them some kind of gift or reward following their reviews, they will be more likely to do it again in the future.

9

DELIGHTING VISITORS
ONE AT A TIME

A ccording to Web guru and trainer Terry Brock, on the Web at TerryBrock.com, you should "focus on the relationships of business, not the electronics of it." Brock contends that we live in an e-crazed world. Everywhere you turn you hear about e-this and e-that. Seems that some are thinking you only have to put an e in front of a word and you are in the digital age.

The technology of 100 years ago was amazing at its time but it still required the human connection. One hundred years from today we'll use technology that will make

> N o matter how sophisticated our technology becomes, we still are working with human beings. This is something the wise and successful businessperson knows.

our latest MP3 files and miniature chips in cellular phones look like 12th century crossbows.

IT'S NOT ABOUT E-COMMERCE; IT'S ABOUT R-COMMERCE

In spite of all the e-commerce, real success comes from r-commerce or relationship commerce. It is the relationship that you have with the customer that matters most. Yes, this is more important than the price. Price can bring in a transaction. It can work for a short time, but it is the long-term relationships you establish that will keep customers coming back again and again. If you base your business on price alone, you'll be blown out of the water when the next new business comes along that can undercut you (and it will eventually).

Case in point: Amazon.com is still viewed as the poster child of e-commerce. Jeff Bezos was *Time* magazine's Man of the Year in 2000 because of the changes he brought to our way of life. The company has focused on helping customers feel comfortable purchasing books, CDs, videos, gifts, and now even furniture. Who knows what it will add in the future?

Is Amazon.com's success due to the fact that it has the lowest prices? Anyone who can click to one of Amazon.com's competitors knows that you can often buy the same product cheaper elsewhere. In the age of clicking to competitors, why doesn't everyone leave Amazon.com in a mouse click and go to the competition?

In the age of sophisticated price shopping robots (like MySimon.com, priceworld.com, and r-u-sure.com), how can Amazon.com stay in business if it doesn't have the cheapest prices? And yes, profit is a hope for Amazon.com although it is building infrastructure and top-of-mind presence now. The profits are in the picture and will come in the future.

The answer is adaptability. Amazon.com started with books and expanded to other areas that customers like. Is it in the book business? No way. It is in the "making customers giddy with glee" business. Any time you have a question or concern, you can be sure that Amazon staff will handle the issue in short order. Who else can you count on to get back to you quickly every time?

Terry Brock maintains that building and enhancing relationships through technology, personal contact, and meeting customers' needs is what it is all about. It was before, it is now, and it will be that way for the next 100 years.

THE FRIENDLY VOICE OF AUTHORITY

Books, airline tickets, and pornography among other products and services can successfully be sold over the Internet without the use of sales staff. Increasingly, it appears many types of products and services require real live salespeople to complete the sale. Such people are in strong demand to provide direction, offer consultation, ask questions, and provide the real-time type of assistance that customers need and want.

What kind of sales staff have you assembled to serve the needs of visitors to your site, many of whom will end up phoning you? Is your

There will always be customers who buy primarily on price. More than ever before such customers will have easy opportunities to comparison shop. Yet, many will get burned from online offers that don't pan out. Others will simply not take the time and effort to fill out tedious online forms. Still others have privacy issues.

staff knowledgeable about your full line of products and services? Are they knowledgeable about what else is offered on the Internet so they can intelligently discuss the benefits and features of your products and services, and why it makes sense for customers to do business with you?

Don't underestimate the potential for you and your sales staff to be the friendly, authoritative voice over the phone. When you're able to differentiate your product or services by truly understanding customer needs and making yourself indispensable to them, and combine this with an effective Web site, you and your sales staff can look forward to continued success.

What about when customers in general call you following a visit to your Web site? Is your company prepared to professionally answer the phone? Many small business enterprises are not. In a recent survey conducted by Communication Briefings, 82 percent of respondents indicated that the way a company answers a phone influences their opinion of that company.

When asked which of the following phone practices bother them the most:

- A long, automated phone menu was cited by 42 percent of the respondents.
- Not having the phone answered by the third or fourth ring was noted by 25 percent of respondents.
- Toll-free numbers that were always busy irked 21 percent.

Other bothersome aspects of calling companies included having to endure music or company ads while they wait, reaching a business that had no answering machine after hours, and failing to have calls returned in a timely manner.

Respondents also were asked which of the following employee phone habits bother them the most. Using a hold button without asking was the most bothersome for 34 percent, followed by 30 percent being uninformed; 15 percent poor grammar; 11 percent not saying their own names; and 6 percent mangling the company name. No matter what time and effort you put into devising a fabulous Web site, you are still likely to highly disappoint the customer if your company's ability to field phone calls is poor.

ANSWER YOUR E-MAILS IN EARNEST

E-mail is so integral to convenient communication that e-mail addresses are becoming as common as telephone numbers. People now expect to communicate their needs to the people they're doing business with at any time, without incurring the limitations of voice mail and costs of long-distance phone calls. Yet, it's easy to cancel the benefits of this quick and easy contact by depersonalizing it or, at worst, ignoring it.

"Lands' End is about building relationships with our customers," says Ron Frey, Internet Business Manager. "We're in for the long haul." Customer service is such a core feature of Lands' End's business philosophy that founder Gary Comer declared, "I'll never judge employees for the actions they take on behalf of our customers." This employee empowerment for the benefit of customers is reflected in the company's e-mail policy.

Businesses that go online often don't plan for the amount of e-mail traffic their Web sites will generate and end up antagonizing, instead of ingratiating, customers. E-mail is a great relationship builder if used properly and given the staff and time resources it deserves.

"We try to answer all our e-mail within 24 hours," notes Frey. Lands' End has assigned staff specifically to handle e-mail. Each electronic communication receives a personal reply and is signed by the person answering it. No automatic form-letter e-mails are used.

To answer e-mails one at a time may seem laborious, even painful, yet consider the impact on the customer. "Wow! A real response, somebody out there cares about what I wrote."

The payoff for customers is obvious—the opportunity to communicate their needs and be heard. The benefit for companies is heightened customer satisfaction that ultimately translates into increased sales, feedback that tells you what you're doing right so you can keep doing it, information that tells you what you're doing wrong so that you can make adjustments, and a bit of fun for all involved.

INDIVIDUALIZED E-MAIL CAMPAIGNS

One way to keep the customers coming back is to start an outbound e-mail campaign in which you send out custom messages or newsletters reminding them of your services. To achieve positive results from your e-mail direct marketing, keep the following in mind:

- You need to plan your strategy.
- Know what you want to say, whether it is promoting a special offer or driving traffic to your Web site.
- Anticipate the level of response that you will generate so you can be sure that you have the staff to handle an increase in sales or services.

E-mail campaigns effectively keep your customers informed so that they will use your services again. The mailing list that receives your newsletter or update might consist of the most important customers you have. Rather than sending junk mail to random people, handpick each respondent to receive your message. You can have people subscribe to your mailing list by completing a form that is accessible from your Web site. Remember to make it easy for people to remove themselves from the list if they so desire.

You can also use zaplets to ensure that e-mail recipients who immediately delete your mail are exposed to your site.

ZAP 'EM WITH ZAPLETS

Zaplets are a Web-based communication platform developed by FireDrop.com based in Redwood Shores, California. The technology works by loading an entire Web site inside an e-mail message. Users can open the Web site and explore directly from the e-mail message. If you want to get people to your Web site, zaplets give you the ability to "e-mail" the site to each target.

Creating a zaplet is easy and, for most types, free. You go to the zaplet site, at zaplet.com, and choose the type of zaplet you want to create from a series of menus. For example, you could choose a poll zaplet. You decide what you want to poll your audience on and send out the zaplet to everyone on your e-mail list. It goes to their e-mail boxes and, as your audience responds to the poll, the results are automatically updated in the zaplet for everyone to see. One major benefit is that you don't have thousands of e-mail responses clogging up your inbox. You can also use them to share pictures and hold discussions. For a fee, FireDrop engineers will custom build a zaplet tailored to your small business needs.

When Internet users are online, 96 percent of them spend most of their time working in the e-mail inbox, according to Jupiter Communications. As an entrepreneur, using e-mail to market your business is a great way to reach people where they spend much of their time.

However, because companies have long since recognized this, e-mail inboxes tend to be full of junk e-mail that becomes deleted before it is even read.

Using a technology such as zaplets gives you a unique way to reach customers because Zaplets are interactive e-mails, not static words on a page.

Influencing your customers to participate can increase the response rate to your e-mail advertising and increase page views on your Web site.

EASY TO REMEMBER AND WORTH ACCENTING

Signature software allows you to put a "signature" at the end of every e-mail you send. This signature should include your company's name, postal address, phone and/or fax numbers, any toll-free numbers, and, of course, your Web address. Beyond the signature, you want to put this same information on every letter and direct mass-mailing that your company sends.

Seek to unify your Web address with your e-mail address. This reinforces your site name and makes it even more familiar to your potential customers. With an effective Web address, Internet users will be able to find your site. If you give your customers repeated opportunities to remember your Web site, they will be more likely to visit, too.

EXTRA MILEAGE WITH EVERY E-MAIL

What needs to be included in your signature file, or sig file, and how long the file ought to be has long been a subject of debate. Internet veterans made the (now feeble) claim that a long signature uses up band-width. As the bandwidth issue began to diminish, others said that a long signature is boastful or arrogant and likely to be resented by those who receive it.

The reality is that a signature file is effective for marketing pur-poses and its length can vary widely depending on what you are trying to achieve and who you are trying to reach. Four lines or less can work perfectly if you are already well-established in your market, or if what you have to offer is so instantly recognizable that no description is necessary.

> Within four lines you can fit your name, address, phone number, fax number, URL, catch phrase, and even a product or service name or two.

If you're a retail vendor, after you've presented the essential contact information, you may wish to list the six or eight hot selling products that you have to offer. A consultant or trainer may wish to offer a list of topic areas covered. A PC guru would be wise to list the types of hard-ware and software that they have significant experience with.

As with any e-mailing, if you target your message carefully, theo-retically, the length of your signature is almost immaterial. The party receiving your message wants to hear from you, has need for your prod-uct or service, and wants a lot of information in a hurry. You incur no marketing penalty for having a long signature. Likewise for using alter-native signatures, templates, or whatever touts your services in an extended manner.

Can a long e-mail signature appear as boastful, garish, or unneces-sary? Most assuredly. That's why you want to ensure that however long

> S ome businesses understate what they have to offer and
> employ e-mail signatures that are too short. They are not
> taking advantage of the opportunity to easily educate and
> inform e-mail recipients.

your signature file may be, you have simplified your prose so that you announce what you have to say in the fewest number of words possible while still conveying the meaning that you intend.

Also, work on the format to ensure that recipients using a variety of e-mail software, monitor sizes, and screen sizes will receive your message, including the signature, in a neat, highly readable format. There is nothing worse than inadvertently spewing garbage across someone else's screen, when, with a little trial and error, you could ensure that your signature message lays out appropriately.

ONLINE EXCESSES OR CONVENIENCES TO RECIPIENTS?

Some say that signature files are passé, that they are easily ignored. True, people understand that signatures are an advertisement and often don't bother reading them, unless they want your specific contact details. Still, they have great utility for all the reasons cited above.

If you want actual guidelines as to length, beyond six lines of immediate contact information, try to keep your signature to less than an additional six lines. People have an aversion to excessively long signatures *unless* the information presented serves some actual benefit. People are also weary of e-mail signatures containing extraneous information, particularly pictures created with ASCII characters.

My signature, for example, is long. Some friends say too long. It lists several of my speaking topics, my six most recent books, and three audiovisual products. However, I have the option of installing one of several e-mail signatures per e-mail, as the situation warrants. It is quick and convenient for me as a speaker and author to have this information ready for recipients who might otherwise ask about it. Also, I can truncate any portions of the signature as necessary.

Often, I simply offer my address and a paragraph about my speaking topics, and delete the book and audiovisual product information.

> With many e-mail software applications you can compose a variety of signatures each with identifying names. Hence, you can offer the appropriate signature to specific correspondents.

It takes some time and energy to develop and install these signatures. It also takes a few moments to select the appropriate signature for each e-mail. However, it's more than worth it if your e-mail and your signature meet the needs and expectations of your correspondent. Meeting needs is what effective Internet marketing strategies are all about.

ERRONEOUS E-MAIL SUBJECT LINES

You have seen them all too often; they appear in your inbox, with alarming regularity. I am talking about spam that comes with all kinds of subject lines. As a general rule, you, as well as your target market, instinctively know when to delete such messages in a nano-second without even considering them.

Any message that comes in the subject line referring to sex, money, or reduced airfares can safely be avoided. The same is true for any messages that claim to offer vacation deals, tax relief, or miraculous cures.

If you use the same type of words in your subject heading that spammers use, chances are your e-mail might be discarded before it's even read. Hence, you've lost the time you spent composing the e-mail, and will waste more time seeking a reply from a party who never read your message to begin with. What are the banished words? You know most of these:

- free
- exclusive
- first time
- make money now
- limited-time only
- naked
- incredible
- adults only
- a one-time offer
- act now

In general, don't use any of the following words or phrases in the subject line of your e-mail, if you intend for any intelligent recipient to read it: Free Guide, Cyber Sex, You Were Carefully Chosen, Hot Nymphs, Consolidate Your Loans Now, Make $50,000 in Just Three Days, How to Stop Belching, More Web Hits Instantly, Pay Zero Taxes...Legally, A Friend Gave Us Your Name, With Over Ten Million E-mail Addresses, You Can't Ignore This Offer, Amazing Pet Training System, Grand Cayman Tax Shelters, Fly for Free, Limited Edition, Stop Psoriasis Now, An Urgent Message, Make Money at Home, ANNOUNCING..., Your Dream Vacation Is Waiting, Get into the College of Your Choice, Don't Ignore This, Retire Now, Secrets Now Revealed, Instant Web Site, We Believe You Would Be Interested..., and Lowest Air Fares Ever.

Also avoid subject lines that employ stars, plus signs, equal signs, or other typographical figures used as "art work."

For marketing, the most efficient use of your time when compiling e-mail messages that you want to be read is to offer a vibrant subject line, or short of that, at least a passable one, so that the other party will indeed open up your mail.

Even if you never send out spam-type e-mail subject headings, which is to your credit, you still have to be careful as to what you put into the subject line of the e-mails that you do send. Appropriate subject lines enhance your marketing campaign and increase the probability of a response.

SPAM REWARDS ONLY ONE PARTY

Spam remains the plague of e-mail, not because the messages themselves have impact or result in revenues for the sponsors. They continue because of the people *selling* mailing lists, and because spam-enhancing software is making money.

If I convince you that the 1,500,000 names in my e-mail database will generate great exposure for your XYZ product, you will pay for my services, and your message is sent out. The returns are pitiful, and you are not sure if you will do repeat e-mailing. If I convince you that, as in print advertising, you have to hit targets at least seven times, you try a second and maybe a third time. You aren't making any money; I am. I will find another one like you, to keep my revenues strong.

MAIL THEM YOUR PRINTOUTS

An effective way to influence customers to visit your site draws upon some tried and true marketing techniques. Visit your own site, and make color printouts of key pages. In other words, press the print button so that you, in effect, create a snapshot on paper of your opening screen, and other vital links within your site. The only resources needed here are your time and a color printer. Then, make packages of your collated Web page copies for mailing to key customers and prospects.

Along with the pages themselves, include a note that says something like, "Visit our site now to learn more about XYZ," or "Visit our site now and take advantage of our XYZ offer." Use highlighters, draw arrows, affix stars—anything to offer your recipients easy guides through the pages they receive.

On the receiving end, when the customer or prospect opens your letter, they will be greeted by pages unlike those they normally see in the mail. After all, who is actually sending personalized, color copies from their own Web site to targeted recipients? Hardly anyone. As recipients unfurl the pages, they are greeted by your highlighted sections and special offers. Is it any wonder that the probability of them visiting your site the next time they are online rises dramatically?

As a variation on this theme, if you change your site frequently by updating prices or services, adding new features, adding news and information, or adding tips or recommendations, feel free to copy those pages that change and use them as the envelope stuffers in your mailing. You could be mailing out once or twice a month, or only quarterly, depending on what suits you, and still maintain an effective strategy for generating Web traffic.

10

USING SEARCH ENGINES, APPEALING TO THE WORLD

Putting up a Web site doesn't guarantee more business. Because your company or business has a Web site, you are not necessarily gaining more exposure. You have to steer visitors to your site. Search engines and directories account for 57 percent of visitors to a given Web site. They are the tool to gaining attention on the Internet and reaching prospective customers.

Search engines automatically catalog and index the information on Web pages, while directories use a human being who groups sites by category. The majority of people online use one of these methods to find sites of interest. If you want your site to be easily accessible, make sure that it is registered with the most popular search engines and directories.

Some search engines are supposed to automatically index new sites. However, it is recommended that you manually submit your site to all of them because some only index home pages rather than the whole site. It may take some time, but it is time well spent.

Choosing keywords for your Web page is also an important part of being accessible on the Web, and especially accessible to the right people. When an Internet user conducts a keyword search related to your company or business, you want your Web site to be one of the first ten that the search returns.

> Most people search for phrases rather than words. Make sure that your industry type, business name, and name of your product are listed as keywords, as well as synonyms for each of these.

HOW MIGHT THEY FIND YOU?

If you take time to think about the audience that you are targeting, you may be able to come up with phrases that they would use to search for your service. If your site has more than one page, use different keyword phrases for each and submit them all to the search engines. This will increase the chances that at least one of your pages will appear in the top ten results of some keyword search.

Be specific with your keywords. To judge if they are specific enough, do a search for them yourself and see how many hits you obtain. Use several of the top search engines, such as Lycos, AltaVista, HotBot, Webcrawler, Infoseek, Northern Light, and Excite. If the number of hits is in the ten-thousands or higher, you will want to be more specific. To do this, you might add the name of your state, city, and county, or names of employees, because people often search for businesses in their areas or for specific names.

KEEP YOUR RANKINGS HIGH

Once you've registered your site with the most popular search engines, consistently check to ensure that your rankings are what you want them to be. Because your site appeared in the top ten results of a keyword search two months ago, doesn't mean that those rankings remain the same. Things are constantly changing on the Web, and so you need to constantly change too, if you plan to stay on top. Check your rankings often—on a weekly basis if possible. To save time you can use a search engine position analyzer such as WebPosition or TopDog.com.

Once you achieve high rankings with your page, *avoid* heavy rewriting in order to keep that ranking. Of course you can update your page as you see necessary, since outdated information will decrease your rankings. Don't make any dramatic changes, however, especially in important keywords.

Once you've found keyword phrases that work for you, use them in your meta keyword and description tags. The title of your page needs to contain your most important keyword, if it does not already.

Since each search engine is different, you might want to find out what each one is looking for. To do this you can visit the help section of a search engine site, look at sites that are receiving high rankings, or find a Web site that is devoted to search engine criteria. A recommended site is *A Webmaster's Guide to Search Engines* at zuww.calafia.com/Webmasters.

Once you understand what each of the major sites regards as important, you can create a doorway page tailored to each search engine. SitePromoter can help you with this task. With the HotBot search engine, pages that are more recently submitted automatically receive higher rankings. If your HotBot rankings slip, you might resubmit your page even if it has not been dropped.

S ometimes a change or technique for achieving higher rankings is not condoned by a search engine. If your site is dropped for any such reason, resubmit it right away.

Maintaining high search engine rankings often is not as difficult as obtaining them in the first place, but it is as important. If you monitor and record your search engine positioning on a regular basis and make necessary adjustments, you will surely be in the top ten results for searches related to your keywords.

NEW WAYS FOR CUSTOMERS TO ACCESS YOUR SITE

Tellme Networks based in Palo Alto, California, at Tellme.com, is among many firms developing new ideas on how to deliver information from the Internet to consumers. The company wants to make information usually accessed over the Internet, such as news and weather information, available via voice by calling a toll-free number. Tellme's service relies on information already on the Web. Its computer voice technology and speech recognition services allow it to efficiently deliver the information to consumers.

A computer will retrieve the information the user requests and play it over the phone, using a computer-generated voice. To access information about a local restaurant, a customer dials the toll-free number on their cell phone and says the word "restaurant." After guiding them through a menu of choices over the phone, Tellme's service delivers what information it can find on the Web. Users will be able to access the service free anywhere by dialing the 1-800 number—from cell phones, pay phones, and home phones.

This service could become useful as more and more people come to rely on wireless phones as an essential, everyday tool. The company will earn money through ad sales and e-commerce services.

Is there a way that your business can make your Web site more accessible? For example, you could ensure that users of a service such as Tellme's can navigate your site over the phone. You could contact them and see if your site is easily found through the voice menu options and is navigable.

Perhaps there are other means of accessing your site. Can it be viewed on a cell phone with Internet access? Portable Internet devices are not able to read HTML and are referred to a special site of a business just for them. Can people view your work on an UNIX-based Web browser? These browsers cannot display graphics of any kind and are not navigable by mouse.

I n the new Web-based business world, success depends upon accessibility. As you construct your site, take into consideration how it is accessed now and what might change in the future. With increased visibility and access, your Web site will help your business grow.

SELLING IN A WIRED WORLD

The Massachusetts-based company Toysmart.com sells educational toys over all the world and all over the Web. Having already tackled the e-business market through its Web store, the company revolutionized its customer-care division by installing a similar system to handle these tasks. Traditional tasks, such as processing customer phone calls and answering faxes and e-mails, are handled by employees who access the company system through Web browsers on their desktop computers.

Silknet eBusiness also uses a platform that is designed for use on the Web. Silknet devised a client/server system for toysmart.com's customer-service sector, and then installed a Web browser to access the system. Using the system, employees are able to handle customers' inquiries and provide faster service.

Silknet's system cuts down the average customer care call by two minutes. The system processes calls and faxes through an automatic call distributor, bringing up any previous records for each customer. This allows the customer service representative to review the case of any repeat caller.

If the call is new, the system encodes the call with a category, such as "return," and then directs it to a representative who can process the request. Currently, there is only one e-mail inbox. A representative has to open and manually tag all e-mails before redirecting them to another representative who can handle the situation.

Using this system, the customer-care division is able to easily process customer requests and also track its own performance. By sorting and storing all the information from customer requests, the system can generate reports, helping toysmart.com better serve its patrons.

In the future, Charest says that toysmart.com hopes to implement this same system on the company's Web site, allowing customers to ask questions and receive answers. The company expects that this would decrease the number of traditional customer calls, faxes, and e-mails, thus allowing them to further streamline customer service.

MAKE YOUR WEB SITE INTERNATIONALLY APPEALING

The majority of Internet users are located in the United States but this is quickly changing. Don't overlook the importance of appealing to a foreign market. If your company is interested in international business, your Web site needs to be globally accessible.

Network Wizards statistics reveal that there are millions of Internet host computers in other countries including 750,327 in Australia, 163,890 in Brazil, 140,577 in South Africa, 130,422 in the Russian Federation, 98,798 in Poland, and 83,949 in Mexico. The global reach of the Internet can also be seen in the percentages of households and users per country. For example, Australia has 18 percent of households online and 4.2 million users. Canada has 39 percent online, which is 9.7 million users.

Ireland has 11 percent of households online and 250,000 users, while Spain has only 6.6 percent online, but 2.25 million users. The United States has the majority with 30 percent of households online and 50 million users.

What do all these numbers mean? Your company or business can have targets overseas as long as your site can be easily navigated by an international visitor.

Besides an awareness of the language difference, an international Web site must take into account the cultural differences among its target audiences.

Conventions that seem acceptable to Americans might be offensive in other societies. Certain colors have different effects in different cultures, especially flag colors. There are rivalries in other countries that Americans are not aware of. Using colors on a Web site that are representative of a country's rival guarantees that the site would not be well received. If you are targeting specific countries, a picture of their nation's flag included on your site is a simple, painless way to make international visitors feel more welcome.

> If you are interested in globalizing your site, recognize that there is no such thing as a quick fix. You have to do your research, or find someone who has done theirs.

If the task of accommodating foreign markets seems overwhelming, but the investment profitable, you might need to consider hiring a localization service. These firms will research what is required to localize your Web site to different countries. Whether or not you use their services, do not overlook the possible foreign market that might access your Web site. You may find that a few changes will expand your business over borders and across oceans.

ACHIEVING GLOBAL RECOGNITION

"Only six percent of the world speaks English," says Barry Shurchin, president of Accurate Translation, a localization service in New York City. In today's growing market economy, it is a necessity for many entrepreneurs to become familiar with terms such as *international marketplace* and *global economy*.

What does this mean for the small business just beginning or finding its place on the Internet? Internet-based company Homeowners.com answered that question by making its Web site and services available to the international community in San Francisco, Califonia. Homeowners.com provides its members a place to research, apply for, and secure a mortgage loan. What makes this company unique is its commitment to provide these services to as many people as possible, regardless of their ability to speak English.

To do so, Homeowners.com provides four language versions of its Web site. A relatively simple idea, yet many Internet-based companies, and even larger, global companies, who are only recently coming to the Internet, fail to provide this service to the international community, both in this country and abroad.

Although Homeowners.com only offers its Web site in English, Spanish, Chinese, and Korean, it has expanded its customer-base by allowing a larger community to comfortably use its product. This creates the potential for a substantial increase in yearly earnings by not limiting its user-base to only English-speaking Internet users, a small community indeed!

As for the small businesses using the Internet as a major resource on which to sell their products, Homeowners.com offers a good example. Why limit access to your Web site to only English-speaking people, especially when "internationalizing" your Web site is a relatively small investment that provides the potential for substantial growth? All this investment requires is effort to find someone, maybe a friend, with some language experience who can translate your site and link it to your original, English site. Other translation software that is also available is from Systran, systran.com, which offers display sites in French, German, Italian, Spanish, and Portugese. There are many other vendors as well.

It is important to make links to international pages a prominent feature of your initial page, so that nonEnglish speaking customers do not have to search for the link to their specific languages. By making this simple addition to your Web site, you have expanded your customer base to unlimited potential and have made your company a member of the global market economy.

In closing, remember: each time someone visits your site, the opportunity to gain a long-term satisfied customer, who will also sing your praises to others, becomes possible. The Internet is a powerful medium. Your Web site can be a powerful marketing tool that will dramatically impact the effectiveness and viability of your business.

APPENDIX

INTERNET MARKETING SECRETS TO DOUBLE YOUR EFFECTIVENESS

URL Roster (first mention of respective URLs)

Introduction

Amazon Booksellers	Amazon.com	bookstore, retail items
Yahoo!	Yahoo.com	search engine, portal
eBay	eBay.com	host for merchandise auctioning
Travelocity	Travelocity.com	travel information

Chapter 1

Powells	Powells.com	bookstore
Inside News	Inside.com	media/entertainment news
Freemerchant	Freemerchant.com	Web-store host
Bigstep	Bigstep.com	Web-store host
eCongo	eCongo.com	Web-store host

Storesense	Storesense.com	online shop
BuyItOnline	BuyItOnline.com	online shop
Z-Shops	zShops.com	online shop
Hirequlity	hirequality.com	military job placement
GovWorks	govWorks.com	getting things done with government

Chapter 2

Google	Google.com	search engine
knowthis.com	knowthis.com	Web marketing techniques
KnowMarketing	KnowMarketing.com	marketing information
Advertising Age	Adage.com	advertising news and information
AdWeek	AdWeek.com	advertising news and information
DirectMarketing Online	DirectMarketing-Online.com	information
DirectMarketing News	Dmnews.com	publication, information
Marketing Research Assn.	MRA-Net.org	information on marketing research
E-Marketers Site	Emarketer.com	offers information on marketing research
Business Marketing Assn.	Marketing.org	provides online marketing tips
American Marketing Assn.	AMA.org	provides online marketing tips
Internet Advertising Bureau	IAB.net	provides online marketing tips
Earthlink	Earthlink.com	Internet service provider
estamps	estamps.com	Postage vendor
Ticketron	Ticketron.com	ticket, event sales
PlanetRx	PlanetRX.com	online pharmacy
MySimon	MySimon.com	price comparison and shopping guide

Mentor University	MentorU.com	online training faculty and course
Excite	Excite.com	search engine and portal
Lycos	Lycos.com	search engine and portal
AltaVista	AltaVista.com	business search engine
PayMyBills	PayMyBills.com	electronic bill payer
E-Trade	Etrade.com	stock purchasing services
OnlineConsultant.com	OnlineConsultant.com	online consultant
1-800-FLOWERS	1-800-FLOWERS.com	flower/gift shop
Wall Street Journal	opinionjournal.com	opinion journal
Breathing Space Institute	BreathingSpace.com	author Jeff Davidson's site
Bill Ringle	BillRingle.com	site for professional speaker Bill Ringle
Ecolab	ecolab.com	chemical company
Sweeping Beauties	sweepingbeauties.com	home cleaning services
Munchkin University	munchkin.com	day care facility
Jeff Davidson	JeffDavidson.com	author and speaker Jeff Davidson
Country Watch	CountryWatch.com	economic and political information
Glen Christopher	caal.com	site for Web trainer Glen Christopher
Goto	Goto.com	search engine
Goto Inventory Search	inventory.go2.com/ inventory/Search Suggestion.jhtml	keyword database
FAST.com	FAST.com	search engine
Northern Light	nlsearch.com	search engine
Inktomi.com	Inktomi.com	search engine
Infoseek	Go-Infoseek.com	search engine
Look Smart	LookSmart.com	directory
Lycos	Lycos.com	directory

Open Directory	OpenDirectory.com	directory
Snap	Snap.com	directory
gainwebtraffic.com	gainwebtraffic.com	offers advice on using key words
keywordpnts.htm	keywordpnts.htm	offers advice on using key words
Hotmail	hotmail.com	free email provider
ChapelHillRent.com	ChapelHillRent.com	property rental guide for Chapel Hill, NC
DVD Express	dvdexpress.com	DVD movies sales
Cyberian Outpost sales	outpost.com	software and hardware
GetMedia Inc.	GetMedia.com	allows radio stations to display and sell what they play on their Web site

Chapter 3

Web Developer's Virtual Library	wdvl.com	writing for Web audience
CNN News	CNN.com	world news source
New York Times	NYTimes.com	world renowned news source
Gamelan	Gamelan.com	directory and registry of Java resources

Chapter 4

Antion's Electronic Magazine	www.antion.com/ ezinesubscribe.html	magazine
Antion's Electronic Magazine	linktrade@ antion.com	address for subscribers to receive instructions on trading links
Antion's Electronic Magazine	aweber.com	sign-up for sequential auto responders

Antion's Electronic Magazine	antion.com	Tom Antion's Web site
Auto Responders	autoresponders.com	information on auto responders
HotBot.com	HotBot.com	search engine
AskJeeves.com	AskJeeves.com	search engine
Barnes and Noble	Barnes&Noble.com	bookstore
RealPlayer	RealPlayer.Com	audio and video player
Dr. Tony Alessandra	Alessandra.com	keynote speaker and author
Dr. Tony Alessandra	PlatinumRule.com	alternative site with self-scoring quiz
Webzine Salon	Webzine Salon.com	'zine
Quickchat	quickchat.org	chat room downloads
multicity.com	multicity.com	chat room downloads

Chapter 5

Sound Domain	SoundDomain.com	car-stereo store
JCrew	Jcrew.com	clothing store
Stone Walrus	StoneWalrus.com	shopping guide
LassoBucks	LassoBucks.com	work-exchange cooperative
USA Today	USAToday.com	world news source
Rick Edler	edlergroup.com	advertises real estate services
Clinique	Clinique.com	makeup and beauty product provider
Trusted Universal Standards	TRUSTe.org	grants Internet site certifications in Electronic Transactions
Better Business Bureau	BBBOnline.org	grants Internet site certifications
Netgrocer	netgrocer.com	online grocer

Blue Marlin	bluemarlincorp.com	hat sales, information on the history of baseball

Chapter 6

Site Launch	SiteLaunch.com	free downloads of games, guest books, bulletin board software, etc.
Lifeminders	Lifeminders.com	e-mail reminder service
Global Language Resources	global-language.com	online library of 600 literature classics
Netscape	netscape.com	Internet portal
grandmother-spider.com	grandmother-spider.com	spirituality site
Nerve	nerve.com	erotica magazine
Netpreneur.com	Netpreneur.com	articles, advice for dotcom entrepreneurs
Pier 1 Imports	pier1.com	furniture and accessories store
Crate and Barrel	crateandbarrel.com	retail goods for the home
Kozmo	kozmo.com	video rentals, magazines, CDs, and snacks
GeoCities	geocities.com	Web publishing tools for non-technical users
K-mart's Blue Light	BlueLight.com	free Internet service

Chapter 7

Fool.Com	fool.com	personal investments management forum
Shipper	Shipper.com	same-day shipping services
NowDocs	NowDocs.com	novel copying, courier services for business
Walter Arnold	www.stonecarver.com	Master stone carver Walter Arnold's site
Authorize.net	Authorize.net	gateway to manage credit card transactions

Cybersource.com	Cybersource.com	see above
Signio.com	Signio.com	see above

Chapter 8

Dan Janal	janal.com	international Internet marketer and author
Master Syndicator	master syndicator.com	software to write and install articles on selected Web pages
Webtracker	webtracker.com	visitor tracking service
Webgarage	webgarage.com	visitor tracking service
Dejanews	dejanews.com	guide to news group and discussion topics
Business Wire	businesswire.com	press release medium
PR Newswire	prnewswire.com	press release medium
Nasdaq	nasdaq.com	technology company stock market
Microsoft Investor	investor.msn.com	money management and investment
All Media E-Mail Directory	owt.com/dircon	directory of nearly 12,000 magazines, newspapers, syndicates, radio, and television stations in the U.S. and Canada

Chapter 9

Terry Brock	TerryBrock.com	PC consultant and speaker
Price World	priceworld.com	shopping bot
r-u-sure.com	r-u-sure.com	shopping bot
FireDrop.com	FireDrop.com	software developer
zaplet.com	zaplet.com	Web site offering zaplet menus

Chapter 10

Webcrawler	Webcrawler.com	search engine

WebPosition	WebPosition.com	search engine position analyzer
TopDog.com	TopDog.com	search engine position analyzer
Webmasters Guide to Search Engines	zuww.calafia.com /webmasters	guide to how search engines work
SitePromoter	SitePromoter.com	creating a doorway page tailored to each search engine
Tellme Networks	Tellme.com	novel information delivery from the Internet to consumers
Toysmart.com	toysmart.com	sells educational toys over all the world
Silknet eBusiness	Silknet.com	a client/server system for customer-service
Homeowners.com	Homeowners.com	provides members a place to research, apply for, and secure a mortgage loan

INDEX